A Time for TRUTH

Answers for Troubled Times

ROGER KIRKPATRICK

CROSSBOOKS

CrossBooks™
A Division of LifeWay
1663 Liberty Drive
Bloomington, IN 47403
www.crossbooks.com
Phone: 1-866-879-0502

© 2013 Roger Kirkpatrick. All rights reserved.

No part of this book may be reproduced, stored in a retrieval system, or transmitted by any means without the written permission of the author.

First published by CrossBooks 06/05/2013

ISBN: 978-1-4627-2778-0 (sc)
ISBN: 978-1-4627-2777-3 (hc)
ISBN: 978-1-4627-2779-7 (e)

Library of Congress Control Number: 2013908226

Printed in the United States of America.

This book is printed on acid-free paper.

Scriptures taken from the Holy Bible, New International Version®, NIV®. Copyright © 1973, 1978, 1984, 2011 by Biblica, Inc.™ Used by permission of Zondervan. All rights reserved worldwide. www.zondervan.com The "NIV" and "New International Version" are trademarks registered in the United States Patent and Trademark Office by Biblica, Inc.™

Because of the dynamic nature of the Internet, any web addresses or links contained in this book may have changed since publication and may no longer be valid. The views expressed in this work are solely those of the author and do not necessarily reflect the views of the publisher, and the publisher hereby disclaims any responsibility for them.

To my cherished daughters,
Sherri and Kristi

Contents

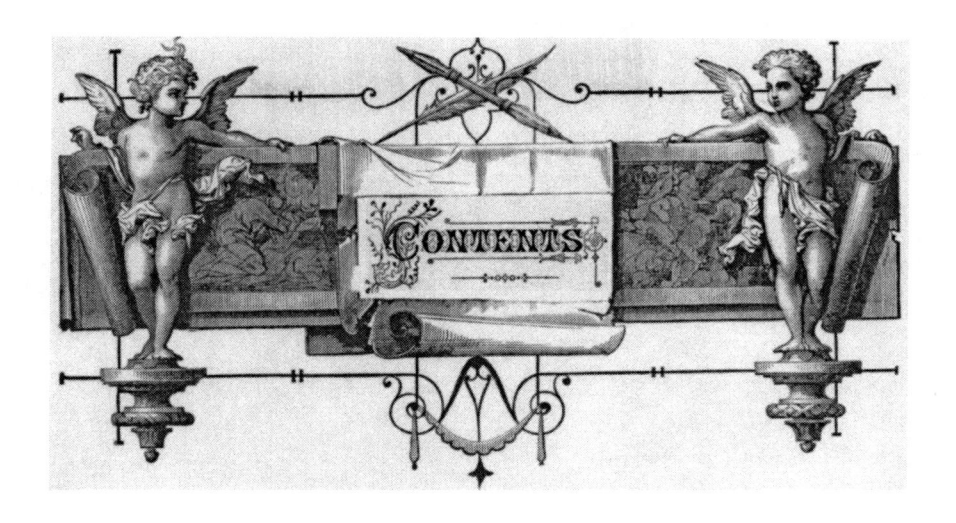

Introduction	xi
Jesus Is the Answer	1
Mind Cannot Traverse the Span	3
The Sovereign Lord	5
The Power Has Come	7
For Me	9
So Great Salvation	16
Faith Is the Hand That Reaches Out	21
Bought, Sought, Brought	23
The Masterpiece	25
Power to Do	27
Enigma	29
Your Worst Enemy	31
Worry	34
Safe and Secure	36
Come Today	38
The Secret Place	41
Do You Know Him?	43
In the Stilly Night	46
The Narrow Gate	48

A Question	51
The Truth	53
My Room	55
My Treasure	57
Nothing Between	60
The Kingdom of My Mind	62
Loved from Eternity	64
Sex	66
Jesus	67
My Help	69
In a Vision of the Night	71
Why I Love Jesus	73
The Sinner's Friend	75
Without Christ	76
Satan's Seminary	78
Preacher, Know Thyself	82
Masquerade	85
Out of Fashion	87
Butchers	90
Legerdemain	92
The Abomination of Desolation	96
Self-Esteem	99
Thank You	101
Dead Men Walking	103
In Him, We Live and Move	105
Only Two Religions	108
Really	110
Crucified	112
Gods	115
Red Letters	118
Fly Away	120
Time	122
Death to a Christian	124
I See the Clouds A-Parting	126
Faith Is the Grace That Yields	128

Little Pebbles	131
Adam	133
Nicodemus	135
Joshua	137
Ship of Fools	139
Darwin	141
A Nation Gone Wrong	144
The Atheist	147
A True Story of Man without God	150
Justification by Faith Alone	152
The Indwelling	157
A Defense of Calvinism	158
The Crown of Life	162

PREFACE

Introduction

This book is an urgent call for you, the reader, to acquaint yourself with the Bible and its Christ. Without Christ, you will be miserable in life and in death.

I am very much aware that dogmatism in our day is out of fashion. Nevertheless, the Bible is a dogmatic book, one that proclaims a certain truth along with a certain and infallible hope.

A mantle of inexplicable darkness is falling upon our world. Evil of every hue envelops the current landscape. Goodness, morality, and truth are fading rapidly into the past, and God's moral laws are being abandoned and trashed. This will not work; God will not be mocked!

The organized church, God's ordained means of recovery, is thrashing about in gross confusion and ignorance. Subjectivism, mysticism, inclusivism, and agnosticism are the hallmarks within multitudes of present-day religious assemblies. As prophesied by the apostle Paul, the great juggernaut of apostasy and the rise of anti-Christian forces are progressing apace. Satan's chains have been loosed; he has gone out to deceive the nations.

We are witnesses to an overall sifting and shaking of the foundations. Great tribulation lies just ahead; this will find its issue in the strengthening and purifying of God's elect people. On the other hand, the ungodly—those who have refused God's overtures of mercy—will be given over, more and more, to their abject obduracy.

Within Christendom, apostate, confused, and deceived leaders are now leading millions to their eternal perdition! If you desire spiritual guidance, turn back to the books of our fathers—Calvin, Luther, Spurgeon, Edwards, and Warfield—and the timeless works of the Puritans. You will be blessed!

God has scattered his holy people throughout all denominations and affiliations. When the last of his elect are gathered in, our Lord will come.

Herein are words of comfort as well as warning. A few of my poems deal with *some* current issues and isms; it would be impossible to deal with all of them, as they are legion. When addressing doctrinal issues, the controversy is not with individuals but with institutions that trample upon, ignore, and twist God's infallible Word.

My desire is to inspire as well as instruct in the doctrines of our holy faith. May God grant his speed to what I have written.

All rhymes are prefaced with a fitting illustration. Many are classic prints and woodcuts from antiquity.

All poems are followed by Scripture-proof texts upon which they are based. Many are embellished by quotes by great and good men, past and present.

Commentary is included in areas where clarification seemed necessary.

All Scripture quotes are from the New International Version of the Holy Bible.

Jesus Is the Answer

That may seem trite,
But it is surely true.
Only he can turn the tide;
He alone can hope renew.

Heavenly philosopher—
Great physician, too.
All other men are liars;
Christ alone is true!

Trust in fleshly wisdom
Has brought us to disaster.
It's time to turn again
To our Lord and Master.

Find within your Bible
Your true and lasting friend.
Pray our God for mercy
To save us once again.

"For the nation or kingdom that will not serve you will perish; it will be utterly ruined" (Isaiah 60:12).

"Should I not avenge myself on such a nation as this?" (Jeremiah 9:9).

"'Return to me, and I will return to you,' says the lord Almighty" (Malachi 3:7).

"Let the wicked forsake his way and the evil man his thoughts. Let him turn to the lord, and he will have mercy on him, and to our God, for he will freely pardon" (Isaiah 55:7).

"But for you who revere my name, the sun of righteousness will rise with healing in its wings" (Malachi 4:2).

> Nor is this spiritual and moral disease to be healed by a better education . . . It requires the hand of the great Physician, the Lord Jesus Christ, by his Holy Spirit, and belief of the truth renewing the state of the mind and disposition of the heart.
> —John Armstrong,
> US Senator (1758-1843)

> History fails to record a single precedent in which nations subject to moral decay have not passed into political and economic decline. There has been either a spiritual awakening to overcome the moral lapse, or a progressive deterioration leading to ultimate national disaster.
> —Douglas MacArthur,
> Five-Star General, World War II

> Go to the Scriptures . . . the joyful promises it contains will be a balsam to all your troubles.
> —Andrew Jackson,
> Seventh President of the United States (1767-1845)

Mind Cannot Traverse the Span

Mind cannot traverse the span
Cleaving God from fallen man.
Till this cataract remove,
I only sip his boundless love:
Mortal knowledge, scant at best,
An ephemeral glimpse, a passing bliss.

In that land where I'll be known
When the mists of night have flown,
Arches of celestial light
Will usher in the morning bright.
In that land of praise, be sure,
Truth shall reign forevermore.

The beatific vision will then o'erflow;
It is then I will fully know
Land of which I've dreamed so long,
Where all is good and I among.
Angel, from the altar fly;
It is thy coming for which I sigh.

"Such knowledge is too wonderful for me, too lofty for me to attain" (Psalm 139:6).

"Now we see but a poor reflection as in a mirror; then we shall see face to face" (1 Corinthians 13:12).

"And I in righteousness I will see your face; when I awake, I will be satisfied with seeing your likeness" (Psalm 17:15).

"We ourselves, who have the first fruits of the Spirit, groan inwardly as we wait eagerly for our adoption as sons, the redemption of our bodies" (Romans 8:23).

> Paul states bluntly that outside of the Christian world there is no hope (1 Thess 4:13) . . . Paul . . . speaks of his own death as a departure (Phil. 1:23). The root meaning of the Greek word is quite interesting. It refers to an "unloosening" and is used of a prisoner who is released. Death is an experience of freedom! . . . The end of physical life is also the moment of deliverance from all sin.
> —Richard Wolff, *The Last Enemy*

> Glorious things of thee are spoken,
> Zion, city of our God;
> He whose word cannot be broken
> Formed thee for His own abode.
> —John Newton

Life is a vapor. Death is an ever-present reality. Myriad are the dangers that threaten our very existence. In Christ alone is found a sure and enduring hope.

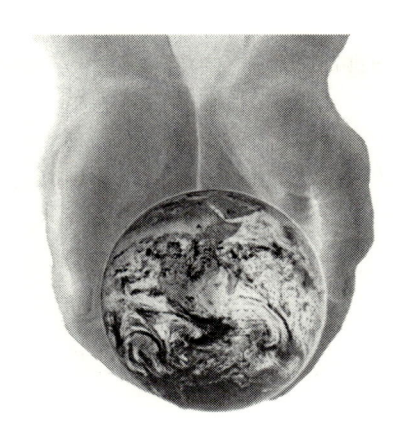

The Sovereign Lord

He cannot fail;
His purposes ever vary.
Though enemies assail,
His plan will not miscarry.

He rules in heaven above
And on the earth below,
And he whose name is love
Will do the right, I know.

The hearts of prince and king
Are guided by his hand.
The sparrow on the wing,
The cattle on the land.

And when disaster falls,
It's from his hand as well.
Angels hearken when he calls,
As well the fiends of hell.

> My heart, fresh courage take.
> Trust where you cannot see.
> He maketh no mistake,
> The one who cares for thee.

"The Lord does whatever pleases him, in the heavens and on the earth, in the seas and all their depths" (Psalm 135:6).

"I say: My purpose will stand, and I will do all that I please" (Isaiah 46:10).

"Jesus . . . said, 'All authority in heaven and on earth has been given to me'" (Matthew 28:18).

"Christ . . . the head over every power and authority" (Colossians 2:10).

"The king's heart is in the hand of the Lord; he directs it like a watercourse wherever he pleases" (Proverbs 21:1).

> God is a sovereign from eternity. He created, because he pleased; he rules in providence as he pleases; he gives grace as he pleases. He asks no opinion. We must with a ready mind, bow down and say Amen.
>
> —J. Clayton, 1811

History is his story. Contrary to public opinion, things are not out of control. Our infinitely wise Creator is carrying out his original design. He is, even now, calling out a chosen people for his name. Wickedness, on the other hand, must reach its full measure so that he may destroy forever a rebellious race.

The Power Has Come

The power of God has come;
That power is in his Son.
He died upon the tree
To set the captives free.

Every living man has a lord;
This we are told in God's Word.
He is either at Satan's behest,
Or he is a slave to righteousness.

Man boasts of his autonomy,
Being all the while not free.
A prisoner of sin from birth,
From sinful seed brought forth.

Unless sin's bands be loosed
By God's almighty grace,
Sin will remain his realm,
Perdition his final place.

"I am not ashamed of the gospel, because it is the power of God for the salvation of everyone who believes" (Romans 1:16).

"We were by nature objects of wrath" (Ephesians 2:3).

"We know that we are children of God, and that the whole world is under the control of the evil one" (1 John 5:19).

"Everyone who calls on the name of the Lord will be saved" (Romans 10:13).

"By grace you have been saved, through faith" (Ephesians 2:8).

Freedom is a term that applies to God alone. Free will is a divine attribute. God alone is absolutely free. Although man boasts of his autonomy, he is, in truth, enslaved to one of two powers.

Saint Augustine explained it this way: man may be compared to a horse with a rider, that rider being either God or Satan and all the while in control of the reins.

Sinful man is born enslaved to evil; hence, he is in desperate need of a deliverer. That is where our Lord Jesus Christ comes in! Amen!

For Me

Left heaven did he—
His throne for me.
Whom angels adored,
By this world abhorred,
Left heaven for me.

Born in a stall was he—
In a lowly stall for me.
He my poverty took,
As foretold in his Book,
Born in a stall for me.

Hated of men was he—
Rejected of men for me.
Despised and forsaken,
By enemies taken,
Hated of men for me

Sweat drops of blood did he,
Praying in Gethsemane.
He pled, "Not my, will but thine."
The cause he pled was mine.
Sweat drops of blood for me.

Made sin was he—
Condemned for me.
He bore my guilt
And my pain felt,
Made sin for me.

Climbed the hill did he—
Calvary's hill for me.
By his Father sent,
Like a lamb he went,
Climbed the hill for me.

Crowned with thorns was he—
His precious head for me.
The blood ran down
And spilt on the ground,
Crowned with thorns for me.

Spat upon was he—
By wicked men for me.
For my disgrace,
They spat in his face,
Spat upon for me.

Stripped of his robes was he—
Mocked and jeered for me.
Put to shame,
And I was to blame,
Stripped of his robes for me.

Lacerated was he—
Crushed and bruised for me.
Beyond recognition
To buy my redemption,
Lacerated for me.

Nailed to the tree was he—
Love held him there for me.
Might have called heaven's host,
Yet alone, he paid the cost.
Nailed to the tree for me.

Died alone did he—
In agony for me.
That's why he came.
Bless his holy name.
Died alone for me.

Shed his blood did he—
His precious blood for me.
What condescension
To bring me salvation,
Shed his blood for me.

Abandoned was he—
Forsaken for me.
On that fateful day,
God turned away,
Abandoned for me.

Laid in the tomb was he—
In the cold tomb for me.
There death held sway
Until the third day;
Then he arose for me.

Conquered death did he—
Vanquished death for me.
That freed from sin,
I might live again,
Conquered death for me.

Bought peace did he—
With God for me.
My iniquity laid
On him was paid,
Bought peace for me.

Ascended on high is he—
At God's right hand for me.
He intercedes
For all my needs,
Ascended on high for me.

Coming again is he—
In the clouds for me.
He'll take me home.
I'll never more roam.
Coming again for me.

Wonderful is he—
So wonderful to me.
I am nothing at all;
He's my all in all,
So wonderful is he to me.

"I came down from heaven" (John 6:42).

"You will find a baby wrapped in cloths and lying in a manger" (Luke 2:12).

"Though he was rich, yet for your sakes he became poor, so that you through his poverty might become rich (2 Corinthians 8:9).

"He was despised and rejected by men" (Isaiah 53:3).

"Jesus went . . . to a place called Gethsemane" (Matthew 26:36).

"Father, if you are willing, take this cup from me; yet not my will, but yours be done" (Luke 22:42).

"It was the Lord's will to crush him" (Isaiah 53:10).

"His sweat became as it were great drops of blood falling down upon the ground" (Luke 22:44).

"God made him who had no sin to be sin for us" (2 Corinthians 5:21).

"Carrying his own cross, he went out to the place of the Skull" (John 19:17).

"He loved us and sent his Son as an atoning sacrifice for our sins" (1 John 4:10).

"He was led like a lamb to the slaughter, and as a sheep before her shearers is silent, so he did not open his mouth" (Isaiah 53:7).

"Twisted together a crown of thorns and set it on his head . . . they spit on him" (Matthew 27:29-30).

"They stripped him and put a scarlet robe on him" (Matthew 27:28).

"Pilate took Jesus and had him flogged" (John 19:1).

"His appearance was so disfigured . . . his form marred beyond human likeness" (Isaiah 52:14).

"He was crushed for our iniquities" (Isaiah 53:5).

"They have pierced my hands and my feet" (Psalm 22:16).

"This is my blood of the covenant . . . poured out for many for the forgiveness of sins" (Matthew 26:28).

"Do you think I cannot call on my Father, and he will at once put at my disposal more than twelve legions of angels?" (Matthew 26:53)

"Jesus cried out in a loud voice . . . 'My God, My God, why have you forsaken me?'" (Matthew 27:46)

"Joseph took the body, wrapped it in a clean linen cloth, and placed it in his own new tomb" (Matthew 27:59-60).

"He is not here; he has risen, just as he said. Come and see the place where he lay" (Matthew 28:6).

"He lives" (2 Corinthians 13:4).

"Because I live, you also will live" (John 14:19).

"Punishment that brought us peace was upon him" (Isaiah 53:5).

"He was taken up into heaven and he sat at the right hand of God" (Mark 16:19).

"Christ Jesus . . . is at the right hand of God and is also interceding for us" (Romans 8:34).

"I am going there to prepare a place for you . . . I will come back and take you to be with me that you also may be where I am" (John 14:2-3).

"Look, he is coming with the clouds, and every eye will see him even those who pierced him; and all the peoples of the earth will mourn because of him. So shall it be! Amen" (Revelation 1:7).

"He will be called Wonderful" (Isaiah 9:6).

My Savior! Fill up the blurred and blotted sketch which my clumsy hand has drawn of a Divine life, with the fullness of thy perfect picture. I feel the beauty I cannot realize; robe me in thine unutterable purity.
—F. W. Robertson

The nature of Christ's existence is mysterious, I admit; but this mystery meets the wants of man. Reject it and the world is an inexplicable riddle; believe it, and the history of our race is satisfactorily explained.
—Napoleon

In the cross of Christ I glory,
Towering o'er the wrecks of time;
All the light of sacred story
Gathers round its head sublime.
—John Bowring

God forbid that we should rejoice in anything but in the cross of Christ.
—Samuel Rutherford, *Letters*

Oh, to have seen Him in the freshness of his resurrection beauty! And what will He be in His glory, when he comes again the second time, and all His holy angels with Him, when He shall sit upon the throne of His glory, and heaven and earth shall flee away before His face.
—C. H. Spurgeon, *Till He Come*

Certain persons would be beautiful were it not for a wound or a bruise, but our Beloved is all the more lovely for His wounds.

—C. H. Spurgeon, Till He Come

So Great Salvation

This two-part rhyme compares what a Christian is in himself or herself to what he or she is in union with Christ.

Part One

"If I must boast, I will boast of the things that show my weakness" (2 Corinthians 11:30).

"Therefore I will boast all the more gladly about my weaknesses, so that Christ's power may rest on me . . . For when I am weak, then I am strong" (2 Corinthians 12:9-10).

"I know that nothing good lives in me" (Romans 7:18).

"Apart from me you can do nothing" (John 15:5).

"I am poor and needy" (Psalm 40:17).

"O my Strength, come quickly to help me" (Psalm 22:19).

Rembrandt's beggar

If I Must Boast

Sinful, wretched, weak, defiled,
Helpless as a little child.
Others boast of purity;
I will boast my need of thee.

Many boast of battles won;
I confess my deeds undone.
Others boast their righteous deeds;
I bemoan my many needs.

I will in my weakness boast,
For it is then you help me most.
In thy strength, I find supply.
Savior, help me, or I die.

At thy fountain, I will sup.
Each new morning, fill my cup.
Sue for help another day,
Strength to help me on my way.

Part Two

"God made him who had no sin to be sin for us, so that in him we might become the righteousness of God" (2 Corinthians 5:21).

"White clothes to wear, so you can cover your shameful nakedness" (Revelation 3:18).

"For in the gospel a righteousness from God is revealed, a righteousness that is by faith from first to last, just as it is written: 'The righteous will live by faith'" (Romans 1:17).

Pure and Whole

Pure and whole, a child of heaven,
Since by grace I've been forgiven.
Covered with a robe of white,
I stand perfected in his sight.

In myself, I'm nothing worth;
In my Lord, I find new birth.
He looks at me, sees only good,
Since I am covered by his blood.

Thus freed from guilt and fear,
I have found a heaven here;
All around is holy ground
Since my Savior I have found.

"How shall we escape if we ignore such a great salvation?" (Hebrews 2:3)

> Thou hast no inherent strength. Know thy strength is perfect weakness. Put on the Lord Jesus Christ.
> —William Mason, *Spiritual Treasury*

> Know where Adam left you; know where the Spirit of God has placed you. Do not know either of these things so exclusively as to forget the other.
> —C. H. Spurgeon, *An All Round Ministry*

The righteousness that all true believers receive upon coming to faith in Christ is twofold. A misunderstanding here is the source of much confusion and discomfort to many. Upon believing, the righteousness of Christ is immediately imputed to the believing soul; from that very moment, he or she stands perfect and whole, exonerated of all guilt in the sight of God. It is this righteousness—and this alone—that entitles the believer to full acceptance and constitutes him or her a recipient of eternal life.

This imputed righteousness, however, is never alone; herein lies the distinguishing mark between a true and false believer. In a genuine conversion experience, the believer is made recipient of an infused righteousness (i.e., the indwelling Holy Spirit). This twofold righteousness constitutes a true saving experience. It is on this point that Scripture gives this admonition: "Examine ourselves to see whether you are in the faith; test yourselves. Do you not realize that Christ Jesus is in you—unless, of course, you fail the test?" (2 Corinthians 13:5)

Again, saving conversion is of supernatural origin. Needless to say, there are many earthly counterfeits. You must be born again (John 3:7).

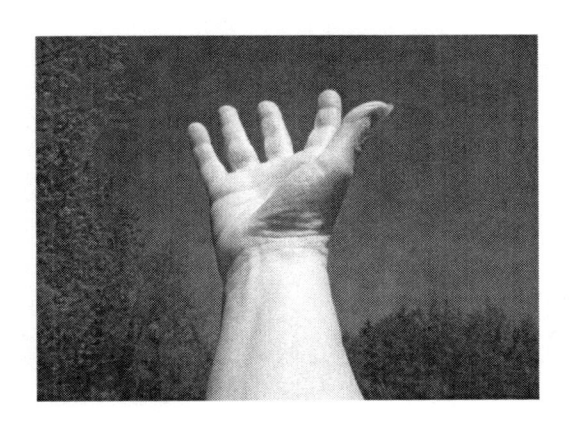

Faith Is the Hand That Reaches Out

Faith is the hand that reaches out—
Takes from the hand of God.
The vital force that lays fast-claim
To a promise in God's Word.

It does no good just to read
Or even to believe;
If it's going to do you good,
My friend, you must receive.

When you see a promise,
Take it—make it your own.
This is the way to victory;
By this, great battles are won.

You see, the battle is in your mind.
Your thoughts are all askew.
You must align your thoughts
To what he's telling you.

"This is the victory that has overcome the world . . . our faith" (1 John 5:4).

"Be strong in the Lord and in his mighty power" (Ephesians 6:10).

"The message they heard was of no value to them, because those who heard did not combine it with faith" (Hebrews 4:2).

"Take captive every thought to make it obedient to Christ" (2 Corinthians 10:5).

> Faith in God is true prudence, but to doubt God is irrational. It is the height of absurdity and folly to question omnipotent love.
> —C. H. Spurgeon

> Faith is a grasping of Almighty power; The hand of man laid on the arm of God—The grand and blessed hour in which the things impossible to me become the possible, O Lord, through Thee.
> —A. E. Hamilton

> Orthodoxy can be learnt from others; living faith must be a matter of personal experience.
> —Buchsel

> Belief is a truth held in the mind; faith is a fire in the heart.
> —Joseph Fort Newton

Faith is believing what God tells us in his Word and acting upon it.

Bought, Sought, Brought

So great salvation the Savior brings;
That is the reason my heart sings.
First he bought us with his own blood
From condemnation in which we stood.

Then he sought us in our misery
Until he found us, you and me;
Last, he brought us from nature's night
Into his kingdom of marvelous light.

Salvation is all of God, my friend.
All glory to him from beginning to end.

"The church of God, which he bought with his own blood" (Acts 20:28).

"The Son of Man came to seek and to save what was lost" (Luke 19:10).

"He has rescued us from the dominion of darkness and brought us into the kingdom of the Son he loves" (Colossians 1:13).

> The thought of the divine initiative in salvation is one of the great doctrines of this Gospel, and indeed of the Christian faith. Men like to feel independent. They think that they come or that they can come to Jesus entirely on their own volition. Jesus assures us that this is an utter impossibility. No man, no man at all can come unless the Father draw him . . . God will teach His people Himself, i.e. He will teach them within their hearts. Only those who are taught in this fashion come to Jesus. But he makes it quite clear that all those who are taught in this way, who hear God, and learn what they hear, do come to Him.
>
> —Leon Morris: Commentary on John 6:44-45

Oh! our hearts loathe the pride which bows not to Divine sovereignty, but arrogantly declares God to be under obligations to his creatures. Those who are full of this satanic spirit will not assert this in plain language, but while they cavil at election, talking with impious breath about "partiality," "injustice," "respect of persons" and such like things, they too plainly show that their old nature is yet unhumbled by Divine grace . . . There is nothing over which the Lord is more jealous than his crown—his sovereignty—his right to do as he will with his own.

—C. H. Spurgeon, *The Saint and His Saviour*

The Masterpiece

I've looked upon
Many a scene
In museum
And magazine—
Portraits sublime, landscapes fair, of untold worth, hanging there.
Yet in my spirit, I still recall a scene I treasure above them all.
I saw a pole in the sod, and hanging upon it the masterpiece of God.
No other scene
Can e'er compare
To the beauty
Hanging there,
For it was there
Life came to me;
Just one look,
And I was free.
From that scene,
Flowers grow,
Hope revives,
And sorrows go.
Kneeling there beneath the pole, relief has come
to many a soul;
Many a burden, many a care, and many a sin lies
buried there.
Look! He whom angels laud—the dying Lamb—the
masterpiece of God.

"I have come that they may have life, and have it to the full" (John 10:10).

"In his name the nations will put their hope" (Matthew 12:21).

"Turn to me and be saved, all you ends of the earth; for I am God, and there is no other. By myself I have sworn, my mouth has uttered in all integrity a word that will not be revoked: Before me every knee will bow; by me every tongue will swear. They will say of me, 'In the LORD alone are righteousness and strength'" (Isaiah 45:22-24).

"For God so loved the world that he gave his one and only Son, that whoever believes in him shall not perish but have eternal life" (John 3:16).

> It was new to ourselves—surprising, startling, and affecting us strangely, as if it were almost too good to be true—when it first shone, like a beam of heaven's own light, into our dark and troubled spirits, and shed abroad "a peace which passeth all understanding." It will be equally new to our children, and our children's children, when they come to know that they have sins to be forgiven, and souls to be saved.
> —James Buchanan (1804-1870)

The raising of Lazarus, Carl Bloch, 1834-1890

Power to Do

Commands given in God's Word
Are really promises in disguise;
For whatever God commands,
He gives the power to do likewise.

When God speaks, never say, "I can't,"
Say, "By thy grace I will."
Although you cannot in yourself,
With God's help, you'll take the hill.

"Stretch out your hand," Christ said
To a man with a shriveled hand.
The task, impossible to the man,
Was enforced by Christ's command.

And what about dead Lazarus—
What did he do at Christ's shout?
He really didn't have a choice—
Dead Lazarus arose and came out.

We are also told in God's Word,
"All men, everywhere, must repent."
You need only look to God's Lamb;
The power to turn will be sent.

Someday, a voice will be heard.
The blast of a trumpet will sound,
God will command the dead, "Wake up!"
They'll obey and come out of the ground.

All this talk may seem strange
And quite impossible to you,
But it's part of my future plans.
You may not believe it, but I do.

"His divine power has given us everything we need for life and godliness" (2 Peter 1:3).

"The LORD helping me, I will" (Joshua 14:12).

"He went into their synagogue . . . a man with a shriveled hand was there . . . he said to the man, 'Stretch out your hand.' So he stretched it out and it was completely restored" (Matthew 12:9-10, 13).

"Jesus called in a loud voice, 'Lazarus, come out!' The dead man came out" (John 11:43-44).

"He commands all people everywhere to repent" (Acts 17:30).

"For the Lord himself will come down from heaven, with a loud command, with the voice of the archangel and with the trumpet call of God, and the dead in Christ will rise" (1 Thessalonians 4:16).

Enigma

The Christian is an enigma—
One person split in two.
One of them is old;
The other one is new.
He desires what is right,
But he wants the evil, too.

The new part wants the right;
The old part wants to rule.
The new part wants the good;
The old part, by nature, is cruel.
Thus, the old must be kept under;
We must refuse to give it fuel.

If you understand this truth,
The battle is half won,
For the new has been giv'n victory
Through the Father's only Son.
So fight the fight of faith.
Soon, you'll hear God say, "Well done."

"Put off your old self, which is being corrupted by its deceitful desires" (Ephesians 4:22).

"Put on the new self, created to be like God in true righteousness and holiness" (Ephesians 4:24).

"You . . . were called to be free. But do not use your freedom to indulge the sinful nature" (Galatians 5:13).

"Live by the Spirit, and you will not gratify the desires of the sinful nature" (Galatians 5:16).

"Put to death, therefore, whatever belongs to your earthly nature: Sexual immorality, impurity, lust, evil desires" (Colossians 3:5).

"What a wretched man I am! Who will rescue me from this body of death? Thanks be to God—through Jesus Christ our Lord!" (Romans 7:24-25)

> How shall I know whether I am a Christian indeed? Shall I know it by a freedom from all anxieties, or by a deliverance from all sin? No; but by an earnest anxiety about the soul, and an incessant conflict with sin and Satan. A living soul trembles at the Divine judgments; labours to obtain a well-founded hope of peace with God; flees to the Lord Jesus Christ for refuge, and cleaves to him with full purpose of heart.
> —Charles Simeon (1759-1836)

Your Worst Enemy

Allow me to introduce to you
Your worst enemy.
I met mine in my mirror;
He was looking back at me.

Paul talks about him at length
In Romans chapter 7.
Paul says he's always with us,
That there's nothing good in him.

When I want to do the good,
This I always find:
The evil is forever there,
Waging war against my mind.

You see, then, my friend,
Our greatest enemy is us,
And there he will remain
Till we lay him in the dust.

He is unspiritual, a slave to sin,
Making war against the new man—
The Spirit that God gave us
When we were born again.

Hence, the war of faith
Which we are called to fight,
We must keep the body under.
Be strong in the Spirit's might.

Henceforth, we inward groan,
Throughout our earthly stay,
Awaiting redemption of our body
At the resurrection day.

"When I want to do good, evil is right there with me" (Romans 7:21).

"I know that nothing good lives in me" (Romans 7:18).

"I see another law at work in the members of my body, waging war against the law of my mind" (Romans 7:23).

"The law is spiritual; but I am unspiritual, sold as a slave to sin" (Romans 7:14).

"You, however, are controlled not by the sinful nature but by the Spirit, if the Spirit of God lives in you" (Romans 8:9).

"We . . . groan inwardly as we wait eagerly for our Adoption as sons, the redemption of our bodies" (Romans 8:23).

"Live by the Spirit, and you will not gratify the desires of the sinful nature" (Galatians 5:16).

"Fight the good fight of the faith. Take hold of the eternal life" (1 Timothy 6:12).

"Be strong in the Lord and in his mighty power" (Ephesians 6:10).

"Therefore, my dear brothers, stand firm. Let nothing move you. Always give yourselves fully to the work of the Lord, because you know that your labor in the Lord is not in vain" (1 Corinthians 15:58).

> So there are two active laws (principles, or powers) that struggle in man for life and death. The Apostle thus speaks of himself as a warrior (divided) between two laws. But he is not defeated (by the evil lusts), as long as he does not surrender to them, which the carnal man does. Indeed the Apostle here shows that he (as a spiritual man) serves only one law, while he resists the other.
> —Martin Luther on Romans 7:23

> Christian, know your calling: it is to work for God: expect opposition from within and without.
> —William Mason, *Spiritual Treasury*

> Be still, thou unregenerate part,
> Disturb no more my settled heart,
> For I have vow'd (and so will do)
> Thee as a foe still to pursue,
> And combat with thee will and must
> Until I see thee laid in th' dust.
> —Anne Bradstreet, from *Flesh and Spirit*

Worry

Do you want to win over worry?
If so, then listen in.
Start by calling it what it is:
Worrying is sin.

Sin, by definition, is
Disobeying God's command.
God tells us not to worry;
Therefore, to worry is sin.

When cares do come upon you,
God tells you what to do.
He says that if you bring them,
He will carry them for you.

You may also view it this way:
What good does worry do?
In fact, it does much harm,
Takes strength and joy from you.

The root goes deeper yet:
You neglect proposed relief.
You refuse to believe God's Word.
Worry's source is unbelief.

> "Be anxious for nothing," God says;
> Now is the time to start.
> Bring it all—nothing is too small.
> His peace will guard your heart.

"Do not worry" (Matthew 6:25).

"Cast all your anxiety on him because he cares for you" (1 Peter 5:7).

"Do not grieve, for the joy of the LORD is your strength" (Nehemiah 8:10).

"Do not be anxious about anything, but in everything, by prayer and petition, with thanksgiving, present your requests to God and the peace of God, which transcends all understanding, will guard your hearts and your minds in Christ Jesus" (Philippians 4:6-7).

> Unbelief is the shield of every sin.
> —William Jenkyn

> We make our sorrows great under the vain idea that they are too small for the Lord to notice. I believe that our greatest miseries spring from those little worries which we hesitate to bring to our heavenly Father.
> —C. H. Spurgeon, *Till He Come*

> When God says to us, "Give me your load, trust me, what you cannot do, I will do for you," He puts our faith to one of the strongest tests. He never consents to carry our burdens unless we give them to him.
> —T. L. Cuyler

Safe and Secure

When things around seem to overwhelm,
Remember, our pilot is still at the helm.
When all around seems dreary and dark,
Remember, believer, you are in God's ark,

Being carried along, come what may,
Safe and secure, above the fray.
God's promises are his ark to you.
Trust in his Word; he will carry you.

"For in the day of trouble he will keep me safe in his dwelling" (Psalm 27:5).

"Even though I walk through the valley of the shadow of death, I will fear no evil, for you are with me" (Psalm 23:4).

"You will keep in perfect peace him whose mind is steadfast, because he trusts in you" (Isaiah 26:3).

"Life will be brighter than noonday, and darkness will become like morning. You will be secure, because there is hope; you will look about you and take your rest in safety. You will lie down, with no one to make you afraid" (Job 11:17-19).

"As the mountains surround Jerusalem, so the LORD surrounds his people both now and forevermore" (Psalm 125:2).

"I will lie down and sleep in peace, for you alone, O LORD, make me dwell in safety" (Psalm 4:8).

> An eminent Christian of old was dying, he called for his Bible. Finding his sight gone, he asked of one present to turn to Romans chapter 8. "Set my finger" he said on the words "I am persuaded that neither death nor life, nor angels, nor principalities, nor powers, nor things present, nor things to come, Nor height, nor depth, nor any other creature, shall be able to separate us from the love of God, which is in Christ Jesus our Lord. "Now" he said "God be with you, my children; I have breakfasted with you, and shall sup with my Lord Jesus Christ this night;" and so departed.
> —Matthew Henry, *Commentary on the Whole Bible*

Two deadly, erroneous ideas have held from the beginning: that a person, by his or her unaided free will, can perform the inner change that God requires, and that he or she must stand idly by, waiting for God to act. Both are wrong. The Bible teaches neither. In the following rhyme, I deal with both.

Come Today

Two things we don't understand—
The purpose of God, the will of man.
But come together they must:
God's calling and man's trust.

Like Lazarus of old,
After he was dead and cold,
The command of Christ was heard;
Dead Lazarus obeyed the word.

The lesson thus applies:
We, too, like him, must rise.
We must come forth like him;
We must be born again.

The mystery of it all
Is held within the call—
The will and the power that can
Both come with God's command.

Don't look to your faith; look to him,
And salvation you will win.
Only one look to live—
The power he will give.

The very least desire,
He will kindle into a fire.
Breathe the simplest prayer,
And he will meet you there.

Rise, and be healed today.
Come now, without delay.
"To all who come," I hear him say,
"I will never turn away."

———∘∘∘❈∘∘∘———

"You must be born again" (John 3:7).

"All that the Father gives me will come to me, and whoever comes to me I will never drive away" (John 6:37).

"Now is the time of God's favor, now is the day of salvation" (2 Corinthians 6:2).

"He commands all people everywhere to repent" (Acts 17:30).

———∘∘∘❈∘∘∘———

"Decisional Regeneration" differs from "Baptismal Regeneration" only in the fact that it attaches the certainty of the new birth to a different act... The practice of "Decisional Regeneration" in the church must be exposed in order to save men from the damning delusion that because they have "decided" or "signed a card" they are going to heaven and are no longer under the wrath of God.

—James E. Adams, *Decisional Regeneration*

I do not trust in the dead sinner's power to live, but the power of the gospel to make him live... As the apostles commanded lame men to stand, and even dead men to live, so, in the name of Jesus Christ of Nazareth command sinners to turn unto Him, and to live.

—C. H. Spurgeon, *An All Round Ministry*

The Secret Place

There is a secret place
Within this world of care.
There you will find Jesus;
He's quietly waiting there.

You'll find no other place,
No matter how you try.
If you miss the Prince of Peace,
True peace will pass you by.

When by faith you enter,
You'll hear a voice so sweet.
"Come in, my child, and rest;
Lay your burdens at my feet."

Why, why then do you wait?
Millions have come, you know.
Why not you, why not now?
There's no place else to go.

"He who dwells in the shelter of the Most High will rest in the shadow of the Almighty. I will say of the LORD, 'He is my refuge and my fortress, my God, in whom I trust'" (Psalm 91:1-2).

"For to us a child is born . . . he will be called Wonderful Counselor, Mighty God, Everlasting Father, Prince of Peace" (Isaiah 9:6).

"Come to me, all you who are weary and burdened, and I will give you rest" (Matthew 11:28).

"We who have believed enter that rest" (Hebrews 4:3).

"Peace I leave with you; my peace I give you. I do not give to you as the world gives. Do not let your hearts be troubled and do not be afraid" (John 14:27).

"The LORD longs to be gracious to you; he rises to show you compassion" (Isaiah 30:18).

"Come now" (Isaiah 1:18).

> To be out of Christ is misery, weakness and death—in short, it is the bud, of which the full-blown flower is damnation. Apart from Jesus we have nothing save fearful forebodings and terrible remembrances. Out of him all is poverty, woe, sorrow, and destruction.
> —Charles Spurgeon, *The Saint and His Saviour*

Peter's denial of Jesus, Carl Bloch, 1834-1890

Do You Know Him?

Not "Have you been baptized?"
Nor "What church do you go to?"
Rather, "Do you know him?"
Whom to know is life anew.

Millions are deceived
By their own religiousness,
By trusting as they do
In their own righteousness.

Born with eyes that cannot see,
And ears that will not hear,
They do not sense their guilt
Nor the danger awaiting there.

Just as all men are born
Under the wrath of God,
So must all be born again
According to God's Word.

That is the great question.
What is your answer, my friend?
To the one who will not come,
God's wrath remains on him.

Give your eyes no sleep
Nor rest to your mind
Till you are drawn to him
And to his will resigned.

"He will punish those who do not know God and do not obey the gospel of our Lord Jesus" (2 Thessalonians 1:8).

"In the gospel a righteousness from God is revealed" (Romans 1:17).

"I am sending you to them to open their eyes and turn them from darkness to light, and from the power of Satan to God" (Acts 26:17-18).

"Jesus declared, 'I tell you the truth, no one can see the kingdom of God unless he is born again'" (John 3:3).

"Like the rest, we were by nature objects of wrath" (Ephesians 2:3).

"Whoever believes in the Son has eternal life . . . whoever rejects the Son will not see life, for God's wrath remains on him" (John 3:36).

"We who have believed enter that rest" (Hebrews 4:3).

Spiritual knowledge of Christ is a personal knowledge. I cannot know Jesus through someone else's acquaintance with Him. No, I must know Him myself . . .

It is also an intelligent knowledge. I must know him—not some illusive vision of Him—but as the Word reveals Him.

Our knowledge of Him will be an affectionate knowledge, for if I know Him at all, I must love Him. And an ounce of heart knowledge is worth a ton of head knowledge.

It will be a satisfying knowledge. When I know the Savior as my own, my mind will be full to overflowing and will feel I have that which my spirit has always longed to know. He is "the bread of life" and whoever eats of that bread "will never go hungry" (John 6:35).

Spiritual knowledge of Christ is an exciting knowledge, for the more I know of my Beloved, the more I will want to know . . . Like a miser with his treasure, my spiritual gold will make me yearn for more.

In conclusion, this knowledge of Christ Jesus will be the most blessed knowledge I can imagine. In fact, it will be so uplifting that often it will completely carry me above all trials, doubts, and sorrows. And while I enjoy this knowledge, it will be working in me to make me more than "man born of a woman who is of few days and full of trouble" (Job 14:1), for it will clothe me in the immortality of the ever-living Savior and wrap me in His eternal joy.

—C. H. Spurgeon

In the Stilly Night

In the stilly night,
When all is calm and still,
You may hear him speaking
If you will.

We do not hear his voice
Throughout the noisy day;
We cannot hear him speak
Above the worldly fray.

While there alone you lie,
Within your quiet place,
You've only to reach out
And touch his face.

In tenderness, he calls,
His hand upon the gate.
He calls for you to come
And for your coming waits.

He is waiting for you now
There in your little room,
Close as the breath you take.
Whisper, and he will come.

Yet he is very jealous;
He may not forever stay.
To those who reject his love,
He may grieve and go away.

"Be still, and know that I am God" (Psalm 46:10).

"On my bed I remember you; I think of you through the watches of the night" (Psalm 63:6).

"Here I am! I stand at the door and knock. If any one hears my voice and opens the door, I will come in" (Revelation 3:20).

"I opened for my lover, but my lover had left; he was gone. My heart sank at his departure. I looked for him but did not find him. I called him but he did not answer" (Song of Solomon 5:6).

"The LORD, whose name is Jealous, is a jealous God" (Exodus 34:14).

Alas, we have lost all righteousness, holiness, and happiness, in ourselves; but we see all these, with heaven and glory, restored to us in Christ. Oh blessed day! happy hour! joyful moment! When the sight of our inestimably precious Savior first saluted the eyes of our mind and became the object of our faith. It was the beginning of days; yea, our birth-day to eternal blessedness.

—William Mason,
A Spiritual Treasury for the Children of God

The Narrow Gate

There is a narrow gate
That few people find;
It opens upon a narrow way,
Constricted and confined.

There is another gate,
Wide open and beckoning,
Of endless fascination,
The latest and greatest thing.

That way is very pleasant,
Agreeable to flesh and blood.
Just follow the latest fad,
And do what fits your mood.

Many are the hucksters
That feed the mind with poison;
Many a false philosophy
Remands the soul to prison.

Many are the bypaths
With signs to lead astray.
This they have in common:
A quick and easy way.

The narrow way is hard.
It cuts against the grain.
We must leave the old paths,
Never to return again.

Why is that way difficult,
And why so hard to find?
Its source is in the blindness
Of our earthly mind.

Ears that refuse to hear,
Eyes that will not see,
Held in Satan's grasp
Till Christ shall set them free.

The gate is in your soul,
Repentance and faith the key.
The way is ever the same:
"Take up your cross, and follow me."

"Enter through the narrow gate. For wide is the gate and broad is the road that leads to destruction, and many enter through it. But small is the gate and narrow the road that leads to life, and only a few find it" (Matthew 7:13-14).

"For it is time for judgment to begin with the family of God; and if it begins with us, what will the outcome be for those who do not obey the gospel of God? And, "If it is hard for the righteous to be saved, what will become of the ungodly and the sinner?" (1 Peter 4:17-18)

"Watch out for false prophets. They come to you in sheep's clothing, but inwardly they are ferocious wolves" (Matthew 7:15).

"The word is near you; it is in your mouth and in your heart," that is, the word of faith we are proclaiming: that if you confess with your mouth 'Jesus is Lord,' and believe in your heart that God raised him from the dead, you will be saved" (Romans 10:8-9).

"Unless you repent, you too will all perish" (Luke 13:5).

"If anyone would come after me, he must deny himself and take up his cross daily and follow me" (Luke 9:23).

> Repentance then is the great, immediate and pressing duty of all who hear the gospel. They are called upon to forsake their sins and return unto God through Jesus Christ. The neglect of this duty is the rejection of salvation . . . It is one of the Mysteries of redemption, that under the economy of mercy, all duties are Graces. Though repentance is our duty, it is no less the gift of God.
>
> —Charles Hodge, *The Way of Life*

A Question

I have a question; answer if you can.
Just how big is the soul of man?
Quite a question for the mind to scan.
I cannot answer, but the Bible can.

All material things will pass away,
But the soul of man is not made that way.
The soul, being made in the image of God,
Cannot be measured by cubit or rod.

The soul is as wide as infinity
And just as long as eternity.
One more question I'll ask of thee:
Where do you think our int'rest should be?

"The day of the Lord will come like a thief. The heavens will disappear with a roar; the elements will be destroyed by fire, and the earth and everything in it will be laid bare . . . That day will bring about the destruction of the heavens by fire, and the elements will melt in the heat" (2 Peter 3:10-12).

"Then they will go away to eternal punishment, but the righteous to eternal life" (Matthew 25:46).

"What is seen is temporary . . . what is unseen is eternal" (2 Corinthians 4:18).

He that will often put eternity and the world before him, and will dare to look steadfastly at both of them, will find that the more he contemplates them, the former will grow greater and the latter less.
—Colton

The created world is but a small parenthesis in eternity.
—Sir Thomas Brown

Eternity for bubbles proves at last
A senseless bargain.
—William Cowper, *The Task, Book 3*

Or sells eternity to get a toy.
—Shakespeare

Eternity, how long? Imagine a bird being commissioned to remove the earth one tiny grain at a time. Imagine that he be allowed only one grain of sand every hundred years. His job being completed with the passing of eons of time, eternity will have only begun.
—Anonymous

We all, like sheep, have gone astray.

The Truth

Sounds strange, but it's true, forsooth;
No man living seeks after truth.
Man, above all, prefers his delusion.
Rather than truth, he hugs his confusion.

The story of mankind as on earth he trod:
Seeking for happiness without God.
He'll try pleasure, fame, riches, religion,
Being all the while Satan's stool-pigeon.

It's called blindness by him who knows.
He sees men wandering without any clothes,
So he sent his Son on a heavenly mission,
Seeking the lost, bringing salvation.

The mind is too big, the heart is too wide;
Only God can fill it and nothing beside.
When you've come to see your lost condition,
Reach out your hand to your only solution.

"There is no one who understands, no one who seeks God" (Romans 3:11).

"For the Son of Man came to seek and to save what was lost" (Luke 19:10).

"You say, 'I am rich' . . . But you do not realize that you are wretched, pitiful, poor, blind and naked" (Revelation 3:17).

"Salvation is found in no one else, for there is no other name under heaven given to men by which we must be saved" (Acts 4:12).

"Come to me, all you who are weary and burdened, and I will give you rest" (Matthew 11:28).

I fled Him, down the nights and down the days;
I fled Him down the arches of the years;
I fled Him, down the labyrinthine ways
Of my own mind; and in the mist of tears
I hid from Him, and under running laughter.
—Francis Thompson (1859-1907), *The Hound of Heaven*

O love that wilt not let me go,
I rest my weary soul in Thee.
—George Mattheson, 1882

My Room

I've a little room where I love to be,
Where, in expectation, I wait quietly.
I sit in wait for my best friend,
And when he knocks, I let him in.

He shows to me his hands and feet
And speaks to me in tones so sweet;
I lay my head upon his breast,
And there I find a perfect rest.

Why he should loves me so,
I do not understand.
But he says it, I believe it,
And on that, I take my stand.

Then he tells me yet of another room,
Where he will come and take me soon.
If I am dreaming, let me dream on,
For I've perfect peace in God's dear Son.

"When you pray, go into your room, close the door and pray to your Father, who is unseen. Then your Father, who sees what is done in secret, will reward you" (Matthew 6:6).

"Here I am! I stand at the door and knock. If anyone hears my voice and opens the door, I will come in" (Revelation 3:20).

"He showed them his hands and feet" (Luke 24:40).

"I have loved you with an everlasting love" (Jeremiah 31:3).

"In my Father's house are many rooms . . . I am going there to prepare a place for you . . . I will come back and take you to be with me" (John 14:2-3).

"The peace of God, which transcends all understanding, will guard your hearts and your minds in Christ Jesus" (Philippians 4:7).

When Jesus comes, the shadows depart.
> —Inscribed on the wall of a castle in Scotland

To be in heaven is to lean one's head upon the breast of Jesus. You have done it on earth. Then you know what heaven is. To be in heaven is to talk with Jesus, to set at his feet, to let our heart beat against his breast.
> —Unknown

My Treasure

I have found a precious treasure
With a value beyond measure.
Beside a dry and dusty road,
I have struck the mother-lode.

First thing at morn and last at night,
I make my way to the treasure site.
There I sift my treasure through,
Test its metal, and find it true.

I find fresh wonders every day
And many good things I take away.
And adding them to all the rest,
I keep them in my treasure chest.

I may say this to your surprise:
I think I'm the richest man alive.
If you doubt my story reliable,
Go look for yourself in the Holy Bible.

"How much better to get wisdom than gold, to choose understanding rather than silver!" (Proverbs 16:16).

"The ordinances of the LORD are sure and altogether righteous. They are more precious than gold, than much pure gold" (Psalm 19:9-10).

"The law from your mouth is more precious to me than thousands of pieces of silver and gold" (Psalm 119:72).

"The fear of the LORD is the key to this treasure" (Isaiah 33:6).

"I have hidden your word in my heart" (Psalm 119:11).

"The kingdom of heaven is like treasure hidden in a field" (Matthew 13:44).

"We have this treasure in jars of clay" (2 Corinthians 4:7).

2012 was my twenty-fifth year reading through the Bible. I recommend the practice very highly.

> The Bible is a treasure. It contains enough to make us rich for time and eternity. It contains the secret of happy living. It contains the title-deeds of an inheritance incorruptible, and that fadeth not away. It contains the pearl of great price . . . it contains the Savior and the living God himself.
> —Robert Hall

> Every atom of truth is worth a mountain of Gold . . . The more we live in the word, the deeper will be the impression—the more glowing the warmth—the more fruitful the result.
> —Charles Bridges (Queen's College Cambridge)
> *Ecclesiastes*, 1860

Most people are probably not aware that John Quincy Adams, our sixth president and signer of the Declaration of Independence, made it his practice to read through the Bible every year.

In a letter to his son in September of 1811, he wrote, "I have myself, for many years, made it a practice to read through the Bible once every year . . . My custom is, to read four to five chapters every morning immediately after rising from my bed. It employs about an hour of my time."

> Search the Scriptures! The Bible is the book of all others, to be read at all ages, and in all conditions of human life; not to be read once or twice or thrice through, and then laid aside, but to be read in small portions of one or two chapters every day, and never to be intermitted.
> —John Quincy Adams, *New Dictionary of Thoughts*

> One gem from that ocean is worth all the pebbles from earthly streams.
> —Robert McCheyne

> The Bible is a window in this prison-world through which we may look into eternity.
> —Timothy Dwight

> The word of God is solid; it will stand a thousand readings; and the man who has gone over it the most frequently and the most carefully is the surest of finding new wonders there.
> —James Hamilton

> If God is a reality, and the soul is a reality, and you are an immortal being, what are you doing with your Bible shut?
> —Herrick Johnson

> This book will keep you from sin, or sin will keep you from this book.
> —Anonymous

Nothing Between

Nothing between my Lord and I,
He is not bounded by earth or sky.
He's always near, though by eyes unseen—
Nothing between, nothing between.

"I will never leave thee," he has said;
On that pillow, I rest my head.
There I abide, calm and serene—
Nothing between, nothing between.

When storm clouds rise across my way,
In a still, small voice I hear him say,
"Nearer, still nearer, closer lean—
Nothing between, nothing between."

When I pass through death's dark valley,
He has promised to be with me.
He will guide through Jordan's stream—
Nothing between, nothing between.

> And when I stand on heaven's shore,
> I'll be with him forevermore.
> His face will then be clearly seen—
> Nothing between, nothing between.

"Surely I am with you always" (Matthew 28:20).

"Even though I walk through the valley of the shadow of death, I will fear no evil, for you are with me" (Psalm 23:4).

"When you pass through the waters, I will be with you" (Isaiah 43:2).

"We shall see him as he is" (1 John 3:1-2).

> I am persuaded that there is no great actual distance between earth and heaven: the distance lies in our dull minds.
> —C. H. Spurgeon, *Till He Come*

> I like sometimes in prayer, when I do not feel that I can say anything, just to set still, and look up; then faith spiritually desires the well-beloved, and hears His voice in the solemn silence of the mind. Thus we have intercourse with Jesus of a closer sort than any words could possibly express.
> —C. H. Spurgeon, *Till He Come*

You may search the whole wide world, but you will never find a hope like that which is promised in Jesus Christ. He alone is able to make such promises and keep them. The arm of flesh will fail you; he alone can be relied upon for time and eternity.

The Kingdom of My Mind

In the kingdom of my mind,
Such peace and joy therein I find.
I leave the troubled world behind
And find sweet solace there.

No matter how dark the days,
In my kingdom, the sun's ablaze.
I walk through flowered ways,
Above the world of care.

Sweet sounds falling on my ear,
Words of comfort, songs of cheer,
Anthems of angels hov'ring near,
And those around me unaware.

Sweet communion, my God and I—
In my spirit, I mount, I fly.
This my portion till I die,
Then wing my way to heaven fair.

"Though you have not seen him . . . you believe in him and are filled with an inexpressible and glorious joy" (1 Peter 1:8).

"The Spirit himself testifies with our spirit, that we are God's children" (Romans 8:16).

"You turned my wailing into dancing; you removed my sackcloth and clothed me with joy that my heart may sing to you and not be silent. O LORD my God, I will give you thanks forever" (Psalm 30:11-12).

It cannot be denied that some Christians are Christians in name only. The true Christian is a man or woman apart. This person delights in joys that the nominal Christian knows nothing of. In a word, he or she has discovered the true elixir of life; this Christian has come into contact with things eternal. Try and convince this person that he or she is deluded, and this Christian will scorn your incredulity. He or she cannot and will not deny this newfound joy.

> Heav'n above is softer blue,
> Earth around is sweeter green!
> Something lives in every hue
> Christless eyes have never seen.
> —George W. Robinson

He chose us in Him before the creation of the world.

Loved from Eternity

He loved me from eternity—
Was then he set his heart on me.
Before the world's foundation,
He included me in his salvation.

Was then he planned to save the lost,
Came down to me, and paid the cost.
When in darkness, I wandered from him,
In loving-kindness, he drew me in.

And if I go astray, he won't let me go.
He'll not turn away, since he loves me so.
Of this he assures me time after time:
I am his, and he is mine.

I have this assurance, whatever assails:
God is love, and love never fails.

"He chose us in him before the creation of the world" (Ephesians 1:4).

"And we know that in all things God works for the good of those who love him, who have been called according to his purpose. For those God foreknew he also predestined to be conformed to the likeness of his Son, that he might be the firstborn among many brothers. And those he predestined, he also called; those he called, he also justified; those he justified, he also glorified" (Romans 8:28-30).

"I have loved you with an everlasting love; I have drawn you with lovingkindness" (Jeremiah 31:3).

"God is love" (1 John 4:16).

"Love never fails" (1 Corinthians 13:8).

> I believe the doctrine of election, because I am quite certain that, if God had not chosen me, I should never have chosen Him; and I am sure He chose me before I was born, or else He never would have chosen me afterwards; and He must have elected me for reasons unknown to me, for I never could find any reason in myself why He should have looked upon me with special love.
> —C. H. Spurgeon, *Autobiography, Vol. 1*

SEX

Now that I have your attention, I'd like to say this:
God made us male and female; the reason is obvious.
God was wise in doing so, this you must admit.
To try and rearrange it, the pieces just won't fit.

You may call it a different version;
God the Father calls it perversion.
If you persist, you risk God's righteous ire.
He's prepared a place for you—a lake of eternal fire.

"Sodom and Gomorrah . . . gave themselves up to sexual immorality and perversion. They serve as an example of those who suffer the punishment of eternal fire" (Jude 6-7).

"The sexually immoral . . . their place will be in the fiery lake of burning sulfur" (Revelation 21:8).

Scientists concur that there is no such thing as a gay gene. Their findings are that traits could start in the womb and later on be compound by early environmental factors. David agrees with this prognosis: "Surely I was sinful at birth, sinful from the time my mother conceived me" (Psalm 51:5). Human perverseness manifests itself in many different forms. People need to be washed.

Jesus

Jesus, sweet, vital force,
My life and source,
Heavenly magnet ye,
Drawing me up to thee.
Promised never to let me go,
Precious Lord, I love you so!

"I have loved you with an everlasting love; I have drawn you with loving-kindness" (Jeremiah 31:3).

"My sheep listen to my voice; I know them, and they follow me. I give them eternal life, and they shall never perish; no one can snatch them out of my hand" (John 10:27-28).

"Being confident of this, that he who began a good work in you will carry it on to completion until the day of Christ Jesus" (Philippians 1:6).

"The LORD will fulfill [his purpose] for me; your love, O LORD, endures forever" (Psalm 138:8).

"He will keep you strong to the end, so that you will be blameless on the day of our Lord Jesus Christ. God, who has called you into fellowship with his Son Jesus Christ our Lord, is faithful" (1 Corinthians 1:8-9).

"Who shall separate us from the love of Christ? Shall trouble or hardship or persecution or famine or nakedness or danger or sword? No, in all these things we are more than conquerors through him who loved us. For I am convinced that neither death nor life, neither angels nor demons, neither the present nor the future, nor any powers, neither height nor depth, nor anything else in all creation, will be able to separate us from the love of God that is in Christ Jesus our Lord" (Romans 8:35, 37-39).

> Dear believer, truly thou wouldst fall, were he to leave thee to thine own keeping for one moment; but Jesus is able to keep thee from falling. Read the promises, believe them, rest upon them.
>
> —Octavious Winslow,
> *Personal Declension and Revival in the Soul*

My Help
Written upon the death of my wife

Holy Spirit,
Sweet tenant of my breast,
Speak to me in this dark hour;
Give me rest.

Weary and tired,
I wait before thy throne,
No word to comfort or to cheer
Save thine alone.

Giver of the wound,
Dispenser of the cup,
Sovereign Lord of love,
Only you can bind it up.

> My waiting eyes
> Are ever toward thee, Lord;
> I wait and hope in thee alone,
> Resting on thy Word.

"My eyes are fixed on you, O Sovereign LORD; in you I take refuge" (Psalm 141:8).

"We know that in all things God works for the good of those who love him, who have been called according to his purpose" (Romans 8:28).

"My flesh and my heart may fail, but God is the strength of my heart and my portion forever" (Psalm 73:26).

"The LORD gave and the LORD has taken away; may the name of the LORD be praised" (Job 1:21).

A right understanding of God's electing love and predestinating purpose is the greatest of all comforts to the grieving believer. The knowledge that all things are predisposed by a loving God and for our ultimate good is the only adequate pillow on which to rest a grieving head.

> The great Physician now is near,
> The sympathizing Jesus;
> He speaks the drooping heart to cheer,
> Oh, hear the voice of Jesus
> —William Hunter

In a Vision of the Night

In a vision of the night,
I beheld a wondrous sight.
I saw one hanging on a tree,
Dying there in agony.

I watched as devils danced about.
One I could not figure out.
As I moved closer in to see,
I saw in an instant, it was me.

It was by my hand the hammer fell;
It was my hand that held the nail.
It was my sins that crucified;
Because of me, the Savior died.

Then he who hung there on the tree
Cast a saving glance at me;
He darted a glance that cast me down.
I fell to my knees there on the ground.

> I said, "O God, what have I done?
> I have slain thine only Son!"
> "It was my will to crush him," he replied,
> "For by his death you are sanctified."

"It was the LORD's will to crush him and cause him to suffer . . . he poured out his life unto death, and was numbered with the transgressors. For he bore the sin of many, and made intercession for the transgressors" (Isaiah 53:10, 12).

"Without the shedding of blood there is no forgiveness" (Hebrews 9:22).

> O ye who love Him not in your inmost souls, ye are those who mock Him: but you say, "Wherein have I failed to crown Him? Did I not join the church? Have I not said I am a believer?" Oh, if your hearts are not right with you, you have only crowned Him with thorns; if you have not given Him your very soul, you have in awful mockery thrust a scepter of reed into His hand. Your very religion mocks you . . . How can you say you love Him, when your heart is not right with Him? If you have never believed in Him, and repented of sin, and yielded obedience to His command, if you do not own Him in your daily life to be both Lord and King, I charge you lay aside the profession which is so dishonoring to Him. If He be God, serve Him; if He be King, obey Him; if He be neither, then do not profess to be Christians.
> —C. H. Spurgeon, Sermon, *Crown of Thorns*

Why I Love Jesus

O yes, I love him, because of who he is:
God with us, Emanuel, all things made are his.
God of very God, ruler of all things,
The great I Am, who to us, salvation brings.

But I'm thinking now of his humanity—
Made in my likeness, yet from all sin free.
I look and behold such beauty there:
The second Adam, but much more fair.

I admire first his integrity;
Never, no never, did he try to deceive.
Wherever he went, he spoke God's Word;
Obedient to his Father, he only spoke what he heard.

His hands never lifted to harm any soul;
His every deed was to heal and console.
When others reviled, he did not revile too;
He said, "Father, forgive, they know not what they do."

When I behold him, my mouth is stopped.
He's everything that I am not;
Yet he gave me this promise, because I am his.
Someday I'll be like him, for I shall see him as he is.

That's why I love him.

"They will call him Immanuel—which means, 'God with us'" (Matthew 1:23).

"All things were created by him and for him" (Colossians 1:16).

"Before Abraham was born, I am!" (John 8:58)

"God made him who had no sin to be sin for us" (2 Corinthians 5:21).

"'The first man Adam became a living being'; the last Adam, a life-giving spirit" (1 Corinthians 15:45).

"My teaching is not my own. It comes from him who sent me" (John 7:16).

"The Father who sent me commanded me what to say and how to say it" (John 12:49).

"He went around doing good and healing all who were under the power of the devil" (Acts 10:38).

"Jesus said, 'Father, forgive them, for they do not know what they are doing'" (Luke 23:34).

"When he appears, we shall be like him, for We shall see him as he is" (1 John 3:2).

The Sinner's Friend

This may seem bold,
But it's true nonetheless:
If it weren't for us sinners,
Jesus would not exist.

Second person of the trinity,
The Father's only Son,
Would never have left his throne
To become the incarnate one.

A Savior without sinners
Would make no sense at all;
So come now to his throne,
And on him boldly call.

Yes, dear sinner, you qualify;
He came not to condemn,
For it is to you he came
To pay your debt. Amen!

"Jesus is not ashamed to call them brothers" (Hebrews 2:11).

Without Christ

Without him, there'd be no happy ending—
No hope, no heavenward pathway wending;
   No friend to walk with, side by side;
   No peaceful haven in which to glide;

None to answer when trouble befalls,
Only an echo to mock the one who calls;
   No one to calm the aching breast;
   Nor caring bosom on which to rest.

I would close my Bible, my lifelong guide,
Knowing the gospel-writers all had lied.
Back to the old life without my friend;
   Back to my emptiness once again.

Oh, but there is a haven, a pleasant lea,
And outstretched arms waiting for me.
   He is my life, my joy, my all,
   And yes, he answers when I call.

"Call to me and I will answer you" (Jeremiah 33:3).

"Call upon me in the day of trouble; I will deliver you, and you will honor me" (Psalm 50:15).

"Brothers, we do not want you to be ignorant about those who fall asleep, or to grieve like the rest of men, who have no hope. We believe that Jesus died and rose again and so we believe that God will bring with Jesus those who have fallen asleep in him. According to the Lord's own word, we tell you that we who are still alive, who are left till the coming of the Lord, will certainly not precede those who have fallen asleep. For the Lord himself will come down from heaven, with a loud command, with the voice of the archangel and with the trumpet call of God, and the dead in Christ will rise first. After that, we who are still alive and are left will be caught up together with them in the clouds to meet the Lord in the air. And so we will be with the Lord forever. Therefore encourage each other with these words" (1 Thessalonians 4:13-18).

> Ye heaven-born, highly-favored souls, well may ye say, "Time, hasten on; years, roll away; moments, fly swiftly; and bring me to the full enjoyment of my beloved Savior in his kingdom of glory."
>
> —William Mason

Satan's Seminary

Listen up—
Do what I say,
For the prophets of old
Did it this way!

I know what I'm doin'.
I've been at this for ages.
I've trained the best:
False prophets and sages.

Quote plenty of Scripture;
Say, "It is written"—
With these three words,
Your dupes will be smitten.

You must tell 'em
What they wanna hear;
You must schmooze 'em
And tickle their ear.

Not knowing you an enemy,
They'll count you a friend;
By this simple means,
They'll welcome you in.

Of course, you must
Distort the true message;
From here and from there,
Hijack a passage.

Pull from these tricks,
Tried and proven:
Here a verse, there a verse,
All interwoven.

Tell 'em, "God wants you
Rich and well."
Talk about fun things;
Don't mention hell.

Tell 'em anything—
It really don't matter;
They'll eat it all up,
As long as you flatter.

Do what I tell ya.
They'll gladly receive it.
They'll arrive in droves;
You won't believe it.

You see, all they want
Is for someone to say
They can get into heaven
The easy way.

Keep 'em thinkin' that
They're born again
'Cause of words they said
Way back when.

Remember our motto:
"Let no soul escape."
We want them forever
To share in our fate.

"Many false prophets will appear and deceive many people" (Matthew 24:11).

"The prophets are prophesying lies in my name" (Jeremiah 14:14).

"For the time will come when men will not put up with sound doctrine. Instead, to suit their own desires, they will gather around them a great number of teachers to say what their itching ears want to hear. They will turn their ears away from the truth and turn aside to myths" (2 Timothy 4:3-4).

"I know that after I leave, savage wolves will come in among you and will not spare the flock. Even from your own number men will arise and distort the truth in order to draw away disciples after them. So be on your guard" (Acts 20:29-31).

"They say to the seers, 'See no more visions!' and to the prophets, 'Give us no more visions of what is right! Tell us pleasant things, prophesy illusions. Leave this way, get off this path, and stop confronting us with the Holy One of Israel!'" (Isaiah 30:10-11)

> It would be very difficult to say how far a man may go in religion, and yet die in his sins; how much we may look like a child of heaven, and yet be a child of wrath . . . In soul matters a man will need to have all his wits about him, or he will soon deceive his own heart.
> —C. H. Spurgeon

There is a true faith, and there is a false faith. There is a natural faith, and there is a divine faith. There is a manmade faith and a God-given faith. Knowing about Christ and knowing Christ are two different things. There is a professing of Christ, and there is a possessing of Christ.

True faith transforms the life: "If anyone is in Christ, he is a new creation; the old has gone, the new has come!" (2 Corinthians 5:17) True faith is the gift of God: "For it is by grace you have been saved, through faith—and this not from yourselves, it is the gift of God" (Ephesians 2:8).

True faith brings the Holy Spirit into the heart: "Did you receive the Holy Spirit when you believed?" (Acts 19:2) True faith fills the heart with love: "God has poured out his love into our hearts by the Holy Spirit, whom he has given us" (Romans 5:5). True faith is an overcoming faith: "This is the victory that has overcome the world, even our faith" (1 John 5:4).

False faith is not an obedient faith: "Faith without deeds is useless" (James 2:20). False faith is the faith of demons: "You believe that there is one God. Good! Even the demons believe that—and shudder" (James 2:19). "Examine yourselves to see whether you are in the faith; test yourselves. Do you not realize that Christ Jesus is in you—unless, of course, you fail the test?" (2 Corinthians 13:5-6)

Preacher, Know Thyself

When behind the desk you stand,
A dying man to dying men,
Choose with care the things you teach.
Do not the Word of God impeach!

Do not add nor take away,
Or you will answer on that day.
Will your message pass the test?
Or will you perish with the rest?

We are warned time and again:
"Beware the teachings of mere men."
Blind leaders of the blind, they're called,
By the enemy of our souls installed.

They tickle the ears and dazzle the eyes,
But this should come as no surprise,
For Scripture said that they would come—
Wolves with sheepish garments on.

Deceiver and deceived will both pass away
On that awful judgment day
When they both are proved to be
Servants of the enemy.

Preacher, this day, you have a choice
To whom you choose to lend your voice.
There'll be no mercy on that day
To those who've lead poor souls astray.

Fingers will point, and eyes will stare
At the one who led them there
When sentence is passed on them, and thee:
"I know you not, depart from me."

"Do not add to what I command you and do not subtract from it" (Deuteronomy 4:2).

"Leave them; they are blind guides. If a blind man leads a blind man, both will fall into a pit" (Matthew 15:14).

"They will gather around them a great number of teachers to say what their itching ears want to hear" (2 Timothy 4:3).

"Not many of you should presume to be teachers . . . because you know that we who teach will be judged more strictly" (James 3:1).

"But there were also false prophets among the people, just as there will be false teachers among you" (2 Peter 2:1).

"Evil men and impostors will go from bad to worse, deceiving and being deceived" (2 Timothy 3:13).

It were better for me that I had never been born than that I preach to these people carelessly, or keep back any part of my Master's truth. Better to have been a devil than a preacher playing fast and loose with God's word, and by such means working the ruin of the souls of men.

—C. H. Spurgeon

If you want to hear soft falsehoods, go elsewhere: I will have none of your blood on my skirts.

—C. H. Spurgeon

Verily in the cells of eternal condemnation there are heard no yells of horror more appalling than the shrieks of damned ministers. Oh, to have misled men—to have ruined their souls forever!

—C. H. Spurgeon

Chrysostom used to wonder that any minister could be saved, seeing our responsibilities are so great. I am entirely of this same mind.

—C. H. Spurgeon

It is evident that a knowledge of the truth is essential to genuine piety. Error never can under any circumstances produce the effects of truth . . . any defect in our knowledge of the truth must, just so far as the error extends, mar the symmetry of the impression produced . . . There is reason to believe, therefore, that all ignorance of revealed truth, or error respecting it, must be attended with a corresponding defect in the religious exercises of the person. This consideration teaches us the importance of truth, and the duty of increasing daily in the knowledge of our Lord and Saviour Jesus Christ.

—Archibald Alexander, *Thoughts on Religious Experience*

Masquerade

It's not an easy road,
The cross way, my friend;
It's a fight from start to finish.
We must fight if we would win.

Our enemy is real,
Although he can't be seen.
That is where the danger lies:
He works through evil men.

He comes in many garbs,
So unassuming and so sweet.
He appeals to human weakness
Through craftiness and deceit.

Presenting themselves as brothers,
Proclaiming to have new light;
They make the old look foolish,
Their way, the only right.

> It calls for vigilance, dear one,
> To resist the Devil's schemes.
> Cling to Christ, the crucified,
> And to the cross way cling.

"Fight the good fight of the faith. Take hold of the eternal life" (1 Timothy 6:11).

"Even from your own number men will arise and distort the truth in order to draw away disciples after them" (Acts 20:30).

"False apostles, deceitful workmen, masquerading as apostles of Christ. And no wonder, for Satan himself masquerades as an angel of light. It is not surprising, then, if his servants masquerade as servants of righteousness" (2 Corinthians 11:13-15).

"Put on the full armor of God so that you can take your stand against the devil's schemes" (Ephesians 6:11).

"Be self-controlled and alert. Your enemy the devil prowls around like a roaring lion looking for someone to devour" (1 Peter 5:8).

> If it is true, it is not new.
> If it is new, it is not true.
>
> —C. H. Spurgeon

> Errors of theory or doctrine are not so much false statements, as partial statements—Half a truth received, while the corresponding half is unknown or rejected, is a practical falsehood.
>
> —Tyron Edwards, *Dictionary of Thoughts*

Lot fleeing Sodom and Gomorrah

Out of Fashion

To talk of hell is out of fashion.
This is surely a trick of Satan.
The Savior talked about it, you know—
A place you do not want to go.

O, you hear it used in other ways,
A word of curse instead of praise.
They tell you to go there when they're mad
And that they feel like it when they're sad.

The word they use in jokes and jeers
Should never be mentioned without tears,
For many a poor soul is going there,
A land of misery and endless despair,

A dreary land where God in not,
A land that forever hope forgot,
The place of everlasting woe—
The Bible says it; it must be so.

"Sodom and Gomorrah and the surrounding towns gave themselves up to sexual immorality and perversion. They serve as an example of those who suffer the punishment of eternal fire" (Jude 7).

"They will go away to eternal punishment" (Matthew 25:46).

"Do not be afraid of those who kill the body but cannot kill the soul. Rather, be afraid of the One who can destroy both soul and body in hell" (Matthew 10:28).

"If your hand causes you to sin, cut it off. It is better for you to enter life maimed than with two hands to go into hell, where the fire never goes out" (Mark 9:43).

"Their worm does not die, and the fire is not quenched" (Mark 9:48).

Working its way into evangelical circles is a new (yet old) heresy. It says that there is no hell—a denial of a truth taught in Scripture and believed among the orthodox down through the ages. An evangelical minister of a major denomination informed me personally that hell is simply being "zapped out of existence." "Have you ever killed a bug?" he asked. He clapped his hands together sharply to illustrate his point.

> We see every day that our imaginations so strong and our reason so weak, the charms of wealth and power so enchanting, and the belief of future punishments so faint that men find ways to persuade themselves to believe any absurdity, to submit to any prostitution, rather than forgo their wishes and desires. Their reason becomes at last an eloquent advocate on the side of their passions, and they bring themselves to believe that black is white, that vice is virtue, that folly is wisdom and eternity a moment."
> —John Adams (Second US President),
> Diary entry, February 9, 1772

No theological tenant is more important than eternal retribution to those modern nations which, like England, Germany, and the United States, are growing rapidly in riches, luxury, and worldly power. Without it, they will infallibly go down in that vortex of sensuality and wickedness that swallowed up Babylon and Rome.

 —W. G. T. Shedd, *The Doctrine of Endless Punishment*
(1885)

All hope abandon ye who enter here.

 —Dante

Hell is truth seen too late—duty neglected in season.

 —Tyrone Edwards

Jesus Christ is the person who is responsible for the doctrine of Eternal Perdition. He is the being with whom all the opponents of this theological tenant are in conflict. Neither the Christian church, nor the Christian ministry are the authors of it.

 —W. G. T. Shedd, *Dogmatic Theology*

The crux of the problem here comes to view. The orthodox doctrine of inspiration and the doctrine of eternal punishment stand or fall together. The only way to escape the doctrine of eternal punishment is to deny the infallibility of scripture.

 —Harry Buis, *The Doctrine of Eternal Punishment*

Butchers

Let me tell you about a deadly schism:
It goes by the name of dispensationalism.
On the Holy Bible, it places a muzzle;
It turns God's Word into a jigsaw puzzle.

It chops, it slices, and yes, it dices,
Voiding God's Word with its many surmises.
By negating the gospel's wonderful news,
It gives children's bread to apostate Jews.

Truth has a ring, error has a smell—
This error, a stench, its home is in hell!
No way is this teaching legit;
It's time to send it back to the pit!

Dispensationalism is not a minor infraction. It is a serious evil that does violence to all of Scripture. It proudly distinguishes itself from the orthodoxy of the past. Remnants of this error have infiltrated every denomination on the planet. Its "left behind" fabrication is a case in point; Scripture knows nothing of this fictitious invention. However, its crowning error is not to be found in their eschatology but in its soteriology. In this lies a soul-damning error.

Its jaundiced view of Scripture requires mental assent alone to secure our soul's salvation. The high priest of dispensationalism, Lewis Sperry Chafer (former president of Dallas Theological Seminary), has this to say: "To impose a need to surrender the life to God as an added condition of salvation is unreasonable." (*Systematic Theology*, III, 385). Obviously, this pregnant statement does away with the offensive doctrine of repentance.

Dispensationalists boast of a literal interpretation of Scripture. This is a ruse. Their so-called literal handling of Scripture is profuse with assumptions and arbitrary overlays that they freely force upon Scripture. This twisted logic runs rampant throughout their voluminous writings.

> Speaking of the system of dispensationalism as embodied in the notes of the famous and influential Schofield Bible, John Wick Bowman says, "This book represents perhaps the most dangerous heresy currently to be found within Christian circles."
> —James Barr, *Dispensationalism*
>
> If dispensationalism is not a heresy, then nothing is heresy.
> —*Fundamentalism* (Westminster Press, 1978)

For a scholarly refutation of this ubiquitous heresy, consult *Dispensationalism, Today, Yesterday, and Tomorrow* by Curtis I. Crenshaw and Grover Gunn, III. Both authors are former dispensationalists.

Legerdemain

The grandest trick of this generation
Has to do with the resurrection.
Called "the rapture," it just won't stand,
For it deals God's Word with sleight of hand.

The truth, in Scripture, is clear and plain—
That all will end when Christ comes again;
No more waiting nor space to amend;
You fall for a trick if you believe it, my friend.

The end will come with one grand sensation.
The earth will burn up in a great conflagration.
No thousand years, as some suppose,
Will come between to interpose.

It will be no secret, and believe it or not,
It will be very noisy! It will be very hot!
Our duty: be ready; he comes as a thief.
Shelter in Christ is our only retreat.

"The day of the Lord will come like a thief. The heavens will disappear with a roar; the elements will be destroyed by fire, and the earth and everything in it will be laid bare . . . That day will bring about the destruction of the heavens by fire, and the elements will melt in the heat But in keeping with his promise we are looking forward to a new heaven and a new earth, the home of righteousness" (2 Peter 3:10-13).

"Be ready, because the Son of Man will come at an hour when you do not expect him" (Matthew 24:44).

The following is a quote from a Trinity Broadcasting Network edition of a book written by Peter and Patti LaLonde. The title is *Left Behind*.

> If you recently witnessed the disappearance of millions of people from the earth, Patti and I have no doubt that you will be confused and probably frightened beyond imagination. Once your initial panic has subsided, you will have a lot of questions. The purpose of this book is to provide you with the best answers we can give about what your future holds. And *please believe us: there is hope.* (emphasis added)

That, my dear friends, is a lie. *Do not believe it!* The secret rapture teaching is not found in Scripture. The Scriptures plainly teach the immediate destruction of all who are unprepared for Christ's second coming. The Scriptures offer no hope whatsoever to those who are left behind. Those who believe otherwise place hope where Scripture gives no hope.

The apostle Paul said plainly in 2 Thessalonians 1:7-10 the nature of what will happen to those who are unprepared for that dread day:

> This will happen when the Lord Jesus is revealed from heaven in blazing fire with his powerful angels. He will punish those who do not know God and do not obey the gospel

of our Lord Jesus. They will be punished with everlasting destruction and shut out from the presence of the Lord and from the majesty of his power on the day he comes.

Preacher, professor, if you teach two comings of Christ, you had better take another look! Do you not see your danger if that teaching is false? Those lost, left behind souls that you gave false hope will damn you at the judgment day. Be dead sure your teaching is correct. You will most certainly give an account to God on that day.

> Recently I was browsing in a Christian bookstore in Albuquerque, New Mexico. I chatted with the manager long enough to discover that she was an enthusiastic proponent of a pre-tribulation rapture and she naturally assumed that her ideas were shared by the majority of the authors whose books she stocked in the store. Her eyes grew wide with amazement as we toured the isles together and discovered that the vast majority of those volumes were authored by people who believed that the rapture and the second coming were one and would happen after the great tribulation.
> —Dave MacPherson, *The Incredible Cover-Up*

> Now, after years of study and prayer, I am absolutely convinced that there will be no rapture before the Tribulation, but that the Church will undoubtedly be called upon to face the Antichrist, and that Christ will come at the close and not at the beginning of that awful period. I believed the other theory simply because I was taught it by W. E. Blackstone in his book *Jesus is Coming*, the Schofield Reference Bible and prophetic Conferences and Bible Schools; but when I began to search the Scriptures for myself I discovered that there is not a single verse in the Bible that upholds the pre-tribulation theory, but that the uniform teaching of the Word of God is of a post-tribulation rapture.
> —Oswald J. Smith, *Tribulation or Rapture—Which?*

Notice the words in the following quotation: "When I began to search the Scriptures for myself." Therein you have the crux of the issue. Most people do not study the Scriptures; therefore, they are open targets for such gross error. The secret rapture myth is popular for that reason. It is simply assumed to be the truth—and that upon the word of *supposed experts*. The truth is, the secret rapture theory is a popular fad that finds no foundation in Scripture. But like so many other fictions, it's the kind of stuff that folks are fond of embracing.

This fiction of course brings in great profits for the end-time hype peddlers. You may be quite sure that the prognostic river will never cease to flow.

The Abomination of Desolation

The abomination of desolation
Is standing in the holy place,
Defying the God of heaven
And the Son of his grace.

This, the hour of darkness,
The Serpent must reign,
Rising from the abyss,
Released from his chain.

The Dragon will wage his war,
God's saints pursuing,
Breaking, at last, the holy ones,
Heaven's ranks subduing.

Desolations have been determined
Before the saints are freed,
Crushed beneath the beast,
For thus has been decreed.

All then will be completed
God's purpose fulfilled,
For all has been determined
As the Father willed.

The Ancient of Days will come,
The Serpent to retake;
He will then be thrown forever
Into the burning lake.

Saints will possess the kingdom
Prepared by God above,
There to bask forever
In their Father's love.

"He will set up an abomination that causes desolation, until the end that is decreed is poured out on him" (Daniel 9:27).

"And I saw an angel coming down out of heaven . . . He seized the dragon, that ancient serpent, who is the devil, or Satan, and bound him for a thousand years. He threw him into the Abyss . . . to keep him from deceiving the nations anymore until the thousand years were ended" (Revelation 20:1-3).

"When the thousand years are over, Satan will be released from his prison . . . They marched across the breadth of the earth and surrounded the camp of God's people, the city he loves. But fire came down from heaven and devoured them. And the devil, who deceived them, was thrown into the lake of burning sulfur" (Revelation 20:7, 9-10).

"When the power of the holy people has been finally broken, all these things will be completed" (Daniel 12:7).

"The Ancient of Days came and pronounced judgment in favor of the saints of the Most High, and the time came when they possessed the kingdom" (Daniel 7:21-22).

Blessed are those who wash their robes, that they may have the right to the tree of life and may go through the gates into the city" (Revelation 22:14).

"He who testifies to these things says, 'Yes, I am coming soon.' Amen. Come, Lord Jesus" (Revelation 22:20).

> When we . . . shall see that plots and conspiracies, that designs for utter ruin, are laid against God's church all the world over; and that none of the kings, princes, or mighty states of the world, will open their doors, or give them a city for refuge; then is the ruin of Antichrist at hand . . . for then indeed, for a little season, will the church of God be overcome . . . remember that when God's church is absolutely forlorn, and has no hiding place any longer in the world, the kingdom of Antichrist will quickly begin to tumble.
> —John Bunyan, *Of Antichrist, and His Ruin*

> All civilization is rocking, and we are facing collapse, morally, politically, and in every way. I would have thought that surely at this time our urgent message should be, "Flee from the wrath to come."
> —D. Martyn Lloyd-Jones, interview, 1980

Self-Esteem

A parasite has attached itself
To the Christian scheme;
It goes by the unhallowed name
Of *self-esteem*.

The term cannot to the saint apply,
Seeing that he is dead;
The Scripture informs us that
He is alive with Christ instead.

All that the believer was,
Together, with all his sin,
In the very long ago,
Died on the cross with him.

Now hidden with Christ in God,
That old man is gone forever.
The new life he now lives,
He lives by the Savior's power.

> I have for you a question.
> Answer if you deem:
> How can a man, long dead,
> Have one ounce of self-esteem?

"I have been crucified with Christ and I no longer live, but Christ lives in me" (Galatians 2:20).

"For you died, and your life is now hidden with Christ in God" (Colossians 3:3).

"You have been given fullness in Christ" (Colossians 2:10).

The Christian is one who no longer looks within for anything good. The true believer says, along with the apostle Paul, "I know that nothing good lives in me" (Romans 7:18).

Strength, purpose, reassurance, confidence, security, ability—all of these the believer finds abundantly in the Lord Jesus Christ. Again, we agree with Paul: "I can do everything through him who gives me strength" (Philippians 4:13).

Much Christian psychology is not Christian at all. It takes the crown from Christ's head and places it upon the head of fallen people.

The true Christian does not live and feed off himself or herself. He or she looks to Jesus Christ for rich supply. Self-esteem, as applied to the believer, is an idea that is foreign to Scripture.

> Any system that proposes to solve human problems apart from the Bible and the power of the Holy Spirit (as all of these pagan systems, including the self-worth system, do) is automatically condemned by Scripture itself.
>
> —Jay E. Adams, *The Biblical View of Self-Esteem, Self-Love, Self-Image*

Spc. Brett Hyde, Tomb Sentinel,
3rd US Infantry Regiment (The Old Guard),
keeps guard over the Tomb of the Unknown Soldier
during Hurricane Sandy at Arlington National
Cemetery, Virginia, October 29, 2012

Thank You

While walking one morning,
I saw on my way
A truck with this sticker:
"I was there; I did D-Day."

On closer look, I saw him
There behind the wheel;
I said, "Sir, got a minute?
I'd like to tell you how I feel.

"I know that words cannot express
The debt I owe to you
For defending our blest country—
The red, white, and blue.

"But I'd like to thank you
For what you did for me
In leaving home and sweetheart
To sail across the sea.

"I couldn't go, I couldn't fight,
For I was only three
When you left home and sweetheart
And sailed across the sea."

A mild and unassuming man,
He thanked me for the care.
And then with moistened eyes,
I left him sitting there.

Friend, if you should see a vet,
Say a word or two.
Thank him for his sacrifice.
He did it for you, too.

Yes, I was just a little guy,
About the age of three,
When he left home and sweetheart
And sailed across the sea.

"Give everyone what you owe him: . . . if respect, then respect; if honor, then honor" (Romans 13:6-7).

"Greater love has no one than this, that he lay down his life for his friends" (John 15:13).

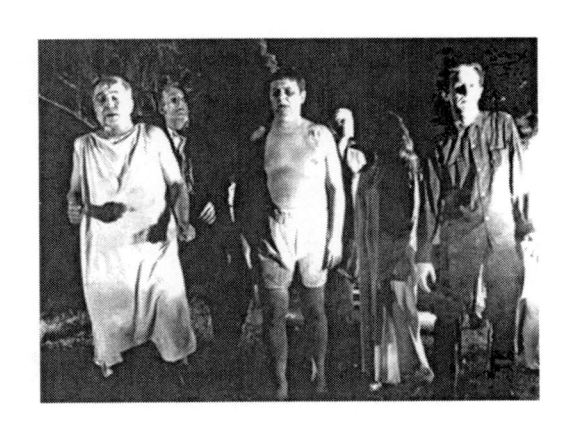

Dead Men Walking

It's a gloomy thought,
But it is true, no doubt:
There's many a dead man
Walking about.

A body in motion,
And a dead soul within it,
May drop to the netherworld
The very next minute.

Into an abyss
Which has no bottom—
A place where hope
Is forever forgotten.

These things, dead men
Don't care to know.
You won't hear about them
On a TV show.

"As for you, you were dead in your transgressions and sins . . . All of us also lived among them at one time . . . But because of his great love for us, God, who is rich in mercy, made us alive with Christ" (Ephesians 2:1-5).

"He who has the Son has life; he who does not have the Son of God does not have life" (1 John 5:12).

"Hell . . . where 'their worm does not die, and the fire is not quenched'" (Mark 9:47-48).

"Give us no more visions of what is right! Tell us pleasant things, prophesy illusions . . . stop confronting us with the Holy One of Israel!" (Isaiah 30:10-11).

"I have come that they may have life, and have it to the full" (John 10:10).

"He who has the Son has life; he who does not have the Son of God does not have life" (1 John 5:12).

"Whoever believes in the Son has eternal life, but whoever rejects the Son will not see life, for God's wrath remains on him" (John 3:36).

"Wake up, O sleeper, rise from the dead, and Christ will shine on you" (Ephesians 5:14).

> I must mourn. I cannot help it. Others may think it enough to mourn over dead bodies. For my part, I think there is far more cause to mourn over dead souls.
> —J. C. Ryle, *Alive or Dead*

In Him, We Live and Move

In him, we live and move
And have our being;
If you are not serving him,
You are stealing.

Created and sustained
By infinite power,
You are in his hand
At this very hour.

You are at his mercy
To do as he will.
He may do you good;
He may bid you ill.

You boast of freedom
You do not possess;
His is a freedom
You cannot resist.

He may at this hour
Withdraw your breath.
His is your life;
His will be your death.

This, the great crime
Of sinful men:
Breathing God's air
While defying him.

Yet mercy is extended,
If you will turn;
If not, there is judgment
At which you will burn.

"For in him we live and move and have our being" (Acts 17:28).

"Know that the LORD is God. It is he who made us, and we are his" (Psalm 100:3).

"We will triumph with our tongues; we own our lips—who is our master?" (Psalm 12:4).

"If it were his intention and he withdrew his spirit and breath, all mankind would perish together and man would return to the dust" (Job 34:14-15).

"Man is destined to die once, and after that to face judgment" (Hebrews 9:27).

"If anyone's name was not found written in the book of life, he was thrown into the lake of fire" (Revelation 20:15).

"Do I take any pleasure in the death of the wicked? declares the Sovereign LORD. Rather, am I not pleased when they turn from their ways and live?" (Ezekiel 18:23)

Let them fear death who do not fear sin.
—Thomas Watson

Only Two Religions

"Only two religions," the Bible says—
One leads to life, the other to death.
The one of life is God's free giving,
The one of death, our own devising.

Whatever moniker you chose to name,
If it's of your doing, it's all the same.
The price of salvation has been paid,
For upon God's Son, all sins were laid.

He is not in contest with the lost;
He will not divide salvation's cost.
He will not be held within your debt;
Salvations terms have all been met.

You must come, as others, to the cross,
Or you will forever rue your loss.
You must give up your manmade plan
And come to the Savior while you can.

"For the wages of sin is death, but the gift of God is eternal life in Christ Jesus our Lord" (Romans 6:23).

"All our righteous acts are like filthy rags" (Isaiah 64:6).

"The LORD has laid on him the iniquity of us all" (Isaiah 53:6).

"He saved us, not because of righteous things we had done but because of his mercy" (Titus 3:5).

"He has appeared once for all at the end of the ages to do away with sin by the sacrifice of himself" (Hebrews 9:26).

"I will not give my glory to another" (Isaiah 42:8).

> God created man in his own image, since then man has been creating a god in his own image.
> —Anonymous

People create in their own minds a comfortable god—one that is easy to live with. But, in time, they will find him extremely hard to die with.

There are only two religions—human religion and God's religion, the religion of works and the religion of grace. The one of people's devising comes in many forms; all amount to the same thing—people working their way to God. God's way has been revealed through Jesus Christ: "No one comes to the Father except through me" (John 14:6). Atoning blood has been shed for the remission of sins. Repentance from dead works and faith in Jesus Christ is the only means of access to the presence of a holy God.

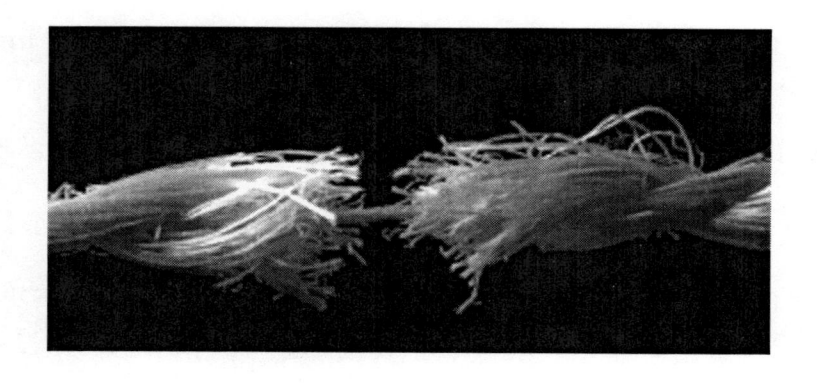

Really

That which is really real,
Physical hands can't feel;
That which is really real,
Faith alone can reveal.

The man without faith
Should surely give pause,
For he's trying to hold on
To a dying cause.

For from this world
And all that is in it,
He could certainly perish
The very next minute.

Thus, eternity will prove
The true foundation
And hope in Christ
Our only salvation.

"All men are like grass, and all their glory is like the flowers of the field; the grass withers and the flowers fall" (1 Peter 1:24-25).

"Death is the destiny of every man; the living should take this to heart" (Ecclesiastes 7:2).

"Each man's life is but a breath. Man is a mere phantom as he goes to and fro" (Psalm 39:5-6).

"So we fix our eyes not on what is seen, but on what is unseen. For what is seen is temporary, but what is unseen is eternal" (2 Corinthians 4:18).

"For here we do not have an enduring city, but we are looking for the city that is to come" (Hebrews 13:14).

> God is real: all else is shadowy. He is certain: all else is questionable.
> —C. H. Spurgeon

> Sense is but short-lived fancy. Faith is reality and substance.
> —William Mason

> This world is all a fleeting show,
> For man's illusion given;
> The smiles of Joy, the tears of Woe,
> Deceitful shine, deceitful flow—
> There's nothing true but Heaven!
>
> —Thomas Moore

Crucified

Christ crucified is not enough
To save your soul from hell;
The Bible says quite plainly,
You must be crucified as well.

Paul tells us in Galatians,
"I have been crucified—
I no longer live—
Christ Jesus lives inside."

All those who belong to Christ
Have been crucified also;
Sinful passions and desires,
They willingly forgo.

The plague throughout the ages:
A believing that does not save,
A faith that will not last
Beyond the grave.

You say that you believe;
The demons believe as well.
The kind of faith they have
Will not save from hell.

Not with the mind alone,
But with your heart and will,
You must submit your all to God.
You will not be saved until.

Christ, indeed, was crucified,
But you must be crucified, too.
Hence the vital question:
Has that ever happened with you?

"Those who belong to Christ Jesus have crucified the sinful nature with its passions and desires" (Galatians 5:24).

"I have been crucified with Christ and I no longer live, but Christ lives in me" (Galatians 2:20).

"You believe that there is one God. Good! Even the demons believe that—and shudder" (James 2:19).

"Here is a trustworthy saying: If we died with him, we will also live with him" (2 Timothy 2:11).

"For you died, and your life is now hidden with Christ in God" (Colossians 3:3).

"For we know that our old self was crucified with him" (Romans 6:6).

"For it is with your heart that you believe and are justified, and it is with your mouth that you confess and are saved" (Romans 10:10).

"Examine yourselves to see whether you are in the faith; test yourselves. Do you not realize that Christ Jesus is in you—unless, of course, you fail the test?" (2 Corinthians 13:5)

It can be said of those who are of Christ that they have crucified the flesh. There came a moment of time in their lives in which they were taken up into that fellowship of life, and in which, therefore, the dominion of the flesh over them was broken.
—H. N. Ridderbos, *Commentary on Galatians*

There is such a thing as being externally in Christ; in him by an avowal of attachment to his cross, by a profession of his name, by adherence to his cause, by an apparent zeal for his glory: all this may exist, and in thousands does exist, without one particle of real, spiritual, life-deriving union to Christ.
—Octavius Winslow,
Personal Declension and Revival in the Soul

All true believers are made partakers with Christ in his death, resurrection, and new life. Hence, the dominion of the sinful nature has been forever broken. Herein lays the distinction between true and false professors.

Gods

Of modern man's obsession with material things

    You show me your god;
    I'll show you mine.
    Mine's always with me;
    I give it all my time.

    O, my friend, that's nothing—
    I have more than one:
    My bosom companions
    From dawn till setting sun.

    I hear they've made a new one
    I cannot wait to try;
    If I don't get my hands on one,
    I think I'll surely die.

But I do have one problem,
And this I must confess—
That when I lay mine down,
I feel an emptiness.

Yes, yes, my friend,
I surely can relate,
For when I lay mine aside,
In my heart, I feel an ache.

Today, I heard this voice:
"Leave them all, and come away."
But as I cannot bear to think,
I just went back to play.

I just hug mine closer
When like thoughts come to me;
Why should I strain my brain
With things I cannot see?

If you think I'll give mine up,
You're really out of your tree.
So when I come to die,
Just throw mine in with me.

"You shall have no other gods before me" (Exodus 20:3).

"Do men make their own gods? Yes" (Jeremiah 16:20).

"The sorrows of those will increase who run after other gods" (Psalm 16:4).

"Dear children, keep yourselves from idols" (1 John 5:21).

"Turn my eyes away from worthless things" (Psalm 119:37).

"Since, then, you have been raised with Christ, set your hearts on things above, where Christ is seated at the right hand of God. Set your minds on things above, not on earthly things" (Colossians 3:1-2).

Men are idolaters, and want something to look at and kiss and hug, or throw themselves down before; they always did, they always will; and if you don't make it out of wood, you must make it out of words.
—Oliver Wendell Holmes

Covetousness implies that the pursuit of earthly possessions is of ultimate significance: It implies that to possess within the finite is a state of fulfillment. This is nonsensical. There is no stability or security in possession within the finite order, where at any moment accident or death may strip or destroy.
—Blamires, *The Secularist Heresy*

I am rather more painfully impressed with the apprehension that the seen world is gaining on the unseen. The vast expansion of its apparatus seems to have nothing to balance it. The Church which was the appointed instrument of the world's recovery, seems, taking all its branches together, rather unequal to its work . . . I am driven back more and more upon the question, "When the Son of man cometh will he find faith upon the earth?" which cannot be frivolous or unmeaning, since it was put by the Saviour.
—William E. Gladstone, Prime Minister of England, in a letter to Sir Thomas Ackland, Dec. 3, 1893

Red Letters

*Written after viewing a coven
of atheists on the Internet*

Prepare your rebuttal,
You despisers of Christ.
Think twice your defenses;
Prepare for the worst.

If he had not come
And did what he did,
If he hadn't spoken
And said what he said,

You would not be guilty.
You would be home free.
But that's not the case,
So listen to me!

Examine very closely
The words he has said;
They will be your judge
On that great day ahead.

Read the red letters.
Let that be your aim.
Study them well,
You base and profane!

For by Christ's words,
You despisers of him,
You will be damned,
And you will be condemned.

You, bring your words;
He'll bring his power.
Your words will crumble;
His might will devour.

"I did not come to judge the world, but to save it. There is a judge for the one who rejects me and does not accept my words; that very word which I spoke will condemn him at the last day" (John 12:47-48).

"He will punish those who do not know God and do not obey the gospel of our Lord Jesus. They will be punished with everlasting destruction and shut out from the presence of the Lord and from the majesty of his power" (2 Thessalonians 1:8-9).

Atheists brag they can get along without God; this is hardly a distinction in an era where very, very few pay the Lord more than a Sunday call.

—Dagobert D. Runes

Fly Away
Based on Psalm 90

We begin our days with a cry;
We end our days with a moan.
Teach me to number my days—
Prepare for my eternal home.

A thousand years to thee
Are like the passing of a day.
Our days are threescore and ten;
They quickly pass—we fly away.

"We finish our years with a moan" (Psalm 90:9).

"Teach us to number our days aright, that we may gain a heart of wisdom" (Psalm 90:12).

"For a thousand years in your sight are like a day that has just gone by" (Psalm 90:4).

"The length of our days is seventy years—or eighty, if we have the strength; yet their span is but trouble and sorrow, for they quickly pass . . . we fly away" (Psalm 90:10).

Psalm 90 is one of the oldest poems in the world. From the remotest times, its authorship has been ascribed to Moses. It is considered one of the most sublime poems ever written. I must also include a most excellent poem by Henry Francis Lyte (1793-1847).

Bird OF My Breast Away

Bird of my breast away!
The long-wish'd hour is come!
On to the realms of cloudless day.
On to thy glorious home!

Long has been thine to mourn
In banishment and pain.
Return, thou wand'ring dove, return,
And find thine ark again!

Away, on joyous wing,
Immensity to range;
Around the throne to soar and sing,
And faith for sight exchange.

Flee, then, from sin and woe,
To joys immortal flee;
Quit thy dark prison-house below,
And be forever free!

I come, ye blessed throng,
Your tasks and joys to share;
O, fill my lips with holy song,
My drooping wing upbear.

Time

The things of time are passing
With the swiftness of a dream;
The things you see and hold
Are not what they seem.

For in a short time passing,
You'll look, and they'll be gone—
The things you worked so hard for,
Those prizes so hard won.

What you see is but a shadow—
A passing show, you know.
Try to hold them if you will.
In time, you'll see them go.

So live for things eternal.
Give them your time and care.
And when you leave this shadow-land,
You'll find them waiting there.

"What is seen is temporary . . . what is unseen is eternal" (2 Corinthians 4:18).

"The world and its desires pass away, but the man who does the will of God lives forever" (1 John 2:17).

A human is distinguished from the animal kingdom only in that he or she has a soul. In that respect, a person is akin to his or her Creator. Because of this blessedness, people are capable of communion with their God. However, the human, the rebellious, has no desire whatsoever for that sacred privilege. A person will set up his or her own god, for sure, but for the true God, this person hasn't the time of day. Fallen and refractory as humanity is, a person would rather wallow in fleshly lust than bow to the Creator God. Carnal pleasures and earthly ambition suit people just fine.

This holds true when things progress smoothly, but when trouble looms, this person is taken aback, and the seeming pleasures lose their hold. Old age and its consequent failures give people pause for regret. The sensual pleasures lose their luster, and if a person has any conscience left, he or she sits like a dunce on a heap of guilt and remorse. The wasted and ignoble creatures, the beasts that people allow themselves to become, find the heavens clouded over, and in a hardened stupor, they slide hopelessly into a Christless eternity. "Today, if you hear his voice, do not harden your hearts" (Hebrews 3:15).

Death to a Christian

Christian, this life is not life,
But a journeying toward life;
Yet to the unbelieving soul,
It's the only life he'll ever know.

That is not death, but life,
Which brings us up to Christ,
For to be absent from here
Is to be present with him there.

This is not life; this is death,
Coming closer with each breath.
This barren land is not our home;
We are seeking a city to come.

Our life is in that city fair;
Many we love are already there.
They will meet us at the gate;
That is the life for which we wait.

"As long as we are at home in the body we are away from the Lord. We are confident, I say, and would prefer to be away from the body and at home with the Lord" (2 Corinthians 5:6, 8).

"For here we do not have an enduring city, but we are looking for the city that is to come" (Hebrews 13:14).

"I am going there to prepare a place for you. And if I go and prepare a place for you, I will come back and take you to be with me that you also may be where I am" (John 14:2-3).

> Death is thy faithful friend . . . it will at once deliver thee from all thy burdens and sorrows, and introduce thee into joys unspeakable and full of glory.
> —William Mason, *A Spiritual Treasury for the Children of God*

> Let thy hope of heaven master thy fear of death, why shouldst thou be afraid to die, who hopest to live by dying.
> —William Gurnall, Puritan

> Let our bodies deteriorate as they will, it can do us no harm, for our body's death is only a passage out of a prison into a palace; out of a sea of troubles into a haven of rest; out of a crowd of enemies into the company of true, loving, and faithful friends; out of shame, bad feelings, and humiliation, into great and eternal glory.
> —John Bunyan, In today's language, Ellyn Sanna

I See the Clouds A-Parting

I see the clouds a-parting now.
I feel the tug of home somehow.
I'm longing for a better place.
I long to see my Savior's face.

Above this world of blackest night,
I see in vision a city bright—
A place where peace and love abound.
In fancy, I hear the joyful sound.

A land of joy and loving smiles,
Peaceful streams, sunlit isles.
Hearts of stone I'll leave behind
To a loving welcome in a better clime.

This is no dream nor rumor heard,
For I've this promise in God's Word.
Sweet angel, come; I welcome you.
Swing wide the gates; I'm coming through.

"They admitted that they were aliens and strangers on earth. People who say such things show that they are looking for a country of their own . . . they were longing for a better country—a heavenly one. Therefore God is not ashamed to be called their God, for he has prepared a city for them" (Hebrews 11:13-14, 16).

"Now we see but a poor reflection as in a mirror; then we shall see face to face" (1 Corinthians 13:12).

"I desire to depart and be with Christ, which is better by far" (Philippians 1:23).

"How blessed are the people who know the joyful sound!" (Psalm 89:15)

"A faith and knowledge resting on the hope of eternal life, which God, who does not lie, promised before the beginning of time" (Titus 1:2).

"Where, O death, is your sting?" (1 Corinthians 15:55)

Heaven, the treasury of everlasting joy.
—Shakespeare

I would not give one moment of heaven for all the joys and riches of the world, even if it lasted for thousands and thousands of years.
—Luther

If I ever reach heaven I expect to find three wonders there: first, to meet some I had not thought to see there; second, to miss some I had expected to see there; and third, the greatest wonder of all, to find myself there.
—John Newton (author of "Amazing Grace")

Faith Is the Grace That Yields

Faith is the grace that yields
To what it cannot understand—
The grace that acquiesces
In our Savior's hidden plan.

All things that happen in time
Were planned of long ago—
Revealed in the Apocalypse
Are some things we may know.

Much will remain a mystery
Until the very end,
But as to our safekeeping,
On God we may depend.

John tells of four great horses
Let loose upon the land.
Of this we must take notice:
They ride at Christ's command.

It is he who breaks the seals,
Sends the steeds upon their way;
It is he who gives them power,
Whose hand no man can stay.

The horses are of color
White, red, black, and pale,
And of Christ we are assured,
Their mission will not fail.

The white is bent on conquest;
He's giv'n pow'r, a bow, and crown.
His is the task of triumphant,
All others to put down.

Another horse goes forth,
This steed, a fiery red.
His rider is given a sword.
By him, much blood is shed.

A black horse is commissioned,
Its rider, with scales, to weigh,
Speaking to us of scarcity,
Of famine and decay.

A pale horse is then released,
And he's given power to kill;
Plague, famine, sword, and death
Are this rider's consummate skill.

Many are the ways of God
That we do not understand;
We must, in childlike faith,
Leave all in our Sovereign's hand.

"I watched as the Lamb opened the . . . seals" (Revelation 6:1).

"War will continue until the end" (Daniel 9:26).

"You will hear of wars and rumors of wars . . . Such things must happen" (Matthew 24:6).

"There will be famines and earthquakes in various places" (Matthew 24:7-8).

"Oh, the depth of the riches of the wisdom and knowledge of God! How unsearchable his judgments, and his paths beyond tracing out!" (Romans 11:33)

"Our God is in heaven; he does whatever pleases him" (Psalm 115:3).

"The Most High is sovereign over the kingdoms of men and gives them to anyone he wishes" (Daniel 4:17).

"All the peoples of the earth are regarded as nothing. He does as he pleases with the powers of heaven and the peoples of the earth. No one can hold back his hand or say to him: 'What have you done?'" (Daniel 4:35).

"Hallelujah! For our Lord God Almighty reigns" (Revelation 19:6).

After each of the delegates had signed the Declaration of Independence, Samuel Adams (1722-1803), father of the Revolution, declared, "We have this day restored the Sovereign to Whom all men out to be obedient. He reigns in heaven and from the rising to the setting of the sun, let His kingdom come."

Little Pebbles

Little pebbles
Can do great things
When by faith and prayer,
God gives them wings.

By feeble servants,
Great deeds are done
When God crowns them
With divine aplomb.

Little David took
A small, smooth stone,
And with God's blessing,
He drove it home.

The lummox fell down,
Cold and dead;
Then David ran, severed
The giant from his head.

> The things you do
> May to you seem small,
> But if they're done in faith,
> God will crown them all.

"Trust in the LORD with all your heart" (Proverbs 3:5).

"My dear brothers, stand firm. Let nothing move you. Always give yourselves fully to the work of the Lord, because you know that your labor in the Lord is not in vain" (1 Corinthians 15:58).

"My word . . . will not return to me empty, but will accomplish what I desire and achieve the purpose for which I sent it" (Isaiah 55:11).

> There is a boundary to the understanding, and when it is reached, faith is the continuation of reason.
> —William Adams

> You cannot be too active as regards your own efforts; you cannot be too dependent as regards Divine grace. Do everything as if God did nothing; depend upon God as if he did everything.
> —John Angel James

Adam

What Adam was and what Adam begun
Is what I am and what I would have done.
God, in his wisdom, put man to the test
To see what he would do without assist.

God turned away and went to his place
To show what man was without his grace.
Man was shown helpless, lost, and undone
And in constant need of the Holy One.

Man thinks he can make it without him;
The only thing he can do without him is sin.
The second Adam came to proffer grace
To a helpless and hopeless, dying race.

With arms outstretched upon a tree,
He lovingly welcomed you and me.
Those who refuse, no other is given—
No other salvation under heaven.

"Just as sin entered the world through one man, and death through sin, and in this way death came to all men, because all sinned" (Romans 5:12).

"For as in Adam all die, so in Christ all will be made alive" (1 Corinthians 15:22).

"The first man Adam became a living being; the last Adam, a life-giving spirit" (1 Corinthians 15:45).

"He who has the Son has life; he who does not have the Son of God does not have life" (1 John 5:12).

"The first man was of the dust of the earth, the second man from heaven" (1 Corinthians 15:47).

"Whoever believes in the Son has eternal life, but whoever rejects the Son will not see life, for God's wrath remains on him" (John 3:36).

> Look at Adam: he too was created in perfect holiness; not a taint of sin originally in his nature; not a cloud darkened his mind; not the least bias of his will, or a single inclination of his heart, but centered in God: and yet, he fell from his original holiness. And why? Because he could not keep himself: God left him to his natural and moral ability, which in the creature is natural and moral weakness, he left him to his own free-will, he left him to his own innate power, and the sad consequence was, he instantly fell, and in him, as their federal head, fell the whole human race.
> —Octavius Winslow, *Personal Declension and Revival in the Soul*

Nicodemus

You've heard about Nicodemus.
As you know, he was no ignoramus—
A religious leader, schooled in the Word,
Teacher of truths which he had heard.

He was wealthy, and he was wise,
But what Jesus said took him by surprise.
This one thing, he did not understand:
"Nicodemus, you must be born again.

"Physical birth, Nicodemus, is not enough.
You must be born of God or be lost.
The Spirit of God must dwell within.
Only he can deliver from sin."

Many are relying on open profession
While knowing nothing of true salvation.
Not having the Spirit of Christ within,
They are without life and still in their sin.

"You must be born again. The wind blows wherever it pleases. You hear its sound, but you cannot tell where it comes from or where it is going. So it is with everyone born of the Spirit" (John 3:7-8).

"If anyone does not have the Spirit of Christ, he does not belong to Christ" (Romans 8:9).

"Examine yourselves to see whether you are in the faith; test yourselves. Do you not realize that Christ Jesus is in you—unless, of course, you fail the test?" (2 Corinthians 13:5)

> It ought always to be remembered that there are two distinct things which the Lord Jesus Christ does for every sinner He undertakes to save. He washes him from his sins in His own blood, and gives him a free pardon:—*this is his justification.* He puts the Holy Spirit into his heart, and makes him an entire new man:—*this is his Regeneration.*
>
> The two things are *both absolutely necessary to salvation.* The change of heart is as necessary as the pardon . . .
>
> The two things are *never separate.* They are never found apart. Every justified man is also a Regenerate man, and every Regenerate man is also a justified man. When the Lord Jesus Christ gives a man remission of sins, He also gives him repentance . . .
>
> There are two great standing maxims of the glorious Gospel, which ought never to be forgotten. One is, "He that believeth not shall be damned." (Mark 16:16.) The other is, "If any man have not the Spirit of Christ, he is none of His." (Rom. 8:9.)
>
> —J. C. Ryle, *A New Birth*

Joshua

You've heard of Joshua and the walls that fell,
Of a greater wonder the scriptures tell.
Joshua was fighting a war one day.
The sun was going down; he told it, "Stay!

"O sun, stand still over Gibeon,
O moon, over the Valley of Aijalon."
He needed more light to rout the foe;
God was fighting for Israel, don't you know?

So the sun stood still the length of a day
So that the enemy could get his pay.
Never before and never again
Has God harkened to the voice of a man.

"Joshua said to the LORD in the presence of Israel:

'O sun, stand still over Gibeon, O moon, over the Valley of Aijalon.' So the sun stood still, and the moon stopped, till the nation avenged itself on its enemies . . . The sun stopped in the middle of the sky and delayed going down about a full day. There has never been a day like it before or since, a day when the LORD listened to a man. Surely the LORD was fighting for Israel!" (Joshua 10:12-14)

"With God all things are possible" (Matthew 19:26).

"What is impossible with men is possible with God" (Luke 18:27).

This miracle is one of the most hotly debated and contested in the entire Bible. On the Internet and in books, you may read for hours the differing opinions of scholars from all disciplines. Trying to solve the riddle of this miracle, as well as any other recorded in Scripture, is an exercise in futility. The fact is that if any one miracle recorded in the Bible could be explained in natural terms, it would no longer be a miracle. We flatter ourselves in attempting to understand the mind and power of our infinite Creator. It takes a thousand times more faith to believe in evolution's mindless creation than to believe and wonder at this wonderful story of Joshua.

Ship of Fools

Ship of state—ship of fools,
Haplessly abandoning God's ten rules.
Code that guided in ages past—
From its tyranny free at last.

Loosed from our moorings, we freely range,
Adrift on a sea of endless change.
If you are honest, you must confess,
This boundless ocean affords no rest.

Hopelessly adrift, O wrenched nation
Since we've abandoned the sure foundation!
Now, since from God we've turned our face,
What will you offer in his place?

"He deprives the leaders of the earth of their reason; he sends them wandering through a trackless waste. They grope in darkness with no light; he makes them stagger like drunkards" (Job 12:24-25).

"'If any nation does not listen, I will completely uproot and destroy it,' declares the LORD" (Jeremiah 12:17).

"If at any time I announce that a nation or kingdom is to be uprooted, torn down and destroyed, and if that nation I warned repents of its evil, then I will relent and not inflict on it the disaster I had planned" (Jeremiah 18:7-8).

"This is what the LORD Almighty says: 'Look! Disaster is spreading from nation to nation; a mighty storm is rising from the ends of the earth'" (Jeremiah 25:32).

"Righteousness exalts a nation, but sin is a disgrace to any people" (Proverbs 14:34).

> If religious books are not widely circulated among the masses in this country, I do not know what is going to become of us as a nation. If truth be not diffused, evil will be; If God and His Word are not known and received, the devil and his works will gain the ascendancy; If the evangelical volume does not reach every hamlet, the pages of a corrupt and licentious literature will; If the power of the gospel is not felt throughout the length and breadth of the land, anarchy and, misrule, degradation and misery, corruption and darkness will reign without mitigation or end.
> —Daniel Webster

> The fate of republican government is indissolubly bound up with the fate of the Christian religion, and a people who reject its holy faith will find themselves the slave of their own evil passions and arbitrary power.
> —Lewis Cass (1782-1866),
> American politician, diplomat

Darwin

Darwin, Schwarwin, Mother Goose—
From such wisdom, turn us loose.
Give children back the God you took;
Give them a hope at which to look.

Tell them of the great Creator
And of his Son, the dying Savior.
Tell them about a heavenly home,
Where they may meet Dad and Mom.

Put godless science in its place.
Ask God to heal our broken race.

"Jesus said, 'Let the little children come to me, and do not hinder them'" (Matthew 19:14-15).

"How often I have longed to gather your children together, as a hen gathers her chicks under her wings, but you were not willing" (Matthew 23:37).

"Jesus said to his disciples, 'Things that cause people to sin are bound to come, but woe to that person through whom they come. It would be better for him to be thrown into the sea with a millstone tied around his neck than for him to cause one of these little ones to sin'" (Luke 17:1-2).

"The blessed hope—the glorious appearing of our great God and Savior, Jesus Christ" (Titus 2:13).

"If my people, who are called by my name, will humble themselves and pray and seek my face and turn from their wicked ways, then will I hear from heaven and will forgive their sin and will heal their land" (2 Chronicles 7:14).

Is it not yet clear the havoc that the godless theory of evolution has wrecked upon our children? Imbecile science, the god of our age, has deceived us. How long before we awaken from our sleep of death? We've tried godlessness, and it doesn't work.

> Our present-day new morality, which would be more accurately labeled "no morality" is the inevitable consequence of such an atheistic philosophy of origins. It is no mere coincidence that the modern deterioration of morality has occurred contemporaneously with the advance of the evolutionary philosophy.
> —Scott M. Huss, PhD

It has become a matter of pride that science is never done: her name is Penelope. But if that is so, then science is not what its founders expected, a source of knowledge; rather, it is an absorbing activity, whose results can never give its patron civilization any conception of the world, much less of that other fugitive, man.

As for the common man, he has been left more than ever at the mercy of his penchant for superstition.

To be sure, science is now wedded to technology and faithful in its service. Many who are close to the work retain their enthusiasm for the future of civilization, precisely because technology can create abundance and replenish or eke out the supply of natural goods. But there are two obstacles on the road to material welfare. One is how to distribute it.

The second and worse barrier to technological blessedness is that it has created conditions of life that more and more people find unendurable. There is no use to rehearse the cries of pain. They form the daily chorus of anguish—in common talk, in the newspapers, in plays and novels, in the grave studies of sociologists and psychiatrists. Against this sort of testimony no argument and no promise will avail. When the sweetness of life, such as it is at the best of times, vanishes altogether, the weak go under and the strong go elsewhere.

If these are not the signs of an emphatic ending, they look uncommonly like it.

—*The Columbia History of the World,*
ed. John Garraty and Peter Gay

A Nation Gone Wrong

Folks mistake the picture;
They've missed by a million miles.
The solution to our problems
Won't be found in Congress aisles.

No government, of itself, is bad.
Evil is in the hearts of men.
Our nation must turn back to God;
Only then can renewal begin.

You say, "God bless America."
Oh really? I think not!
What god are you talkin' about?
Must be one that you made up!

We've broken all his laws,
Insulted him to his face;
Give me one good reason
Why God should bless this place.

This country was founded
By good, God-fearing men;
Only if we turn back to God
Can it be made good again.

I don't believe it will happen
Now that science is our god;
To trust in an unseen power now
Would, to us, seem rather odd.

You see, our leaders no longer
Believe in a divine providence;
The god of political science is
The only deity they countenance.

I believe we are living witness
To our government's great fall;
Like King Belshazzar of old,
The handwriting is on the wall.

"The fingers of a human hand appeared and wrote on the plaster of the wall . . . The king watched the hand as it wrote . . . 'God has numbered the days of your reign and brought it to an end'" (Daniel 5:5, 26).

"The Most High is sovereign over the kingdoms of men and gives them to anyone he wishes" (Daniel 4:17).

"His dominion is an eternal dominion; his kingdom endures from generation to generation. All the peoples of the earth are regarded as nothing. He does as he pleases with the powers of heaven and the peoples of the earth. No one can hold back his hand or say to him: 'What have you done?'" (Daniel 4:34-35)

John Adams, our second president, in an address to the military, said this: "We have no government armed with power capable of contending with human passions unbridled by morality and religion . . . Our Constitution was made only for a moral and religious people. It is wholly inadequate to the government of any other."

> While the people are virtuous they cannot be subdued; but when they lose their virtue they will be ready to surrender their liberties to the first external or internal invader . . . If virtue and knowledge are diffused among the people, they will never be inslaved. This will be their great security.
> —Samuel Adams (1722-1803),
> father of the American Revolution

The following is an excerpt from an article entitled "A Woman Writer Takes A Critical Look At America" from *US News & World Report*, March 2, 1964: "Unless there is a change, deep down, in the American people, a genuine crusade against self-indulgence, immorality public and private, then we are witnesses to the decline and fall of the American Republic."

> Morality, like religion, has the double aspect of satisfying an emotional need and serving a social purpose. Without morality—some inner restraint— society must assign two policemen to watch every citizen day and night. And without a religion which sustains conduct or at least organizes the facts of life and the cosmos, men seek in vain for the meaning of their existence.
> —John Garraty and Peter Gay,
> *The Columbia History of the World*

"The fool says in his heart, 'There is no God.' They are corrupt, and their ways are vile" (Psalm 53:1).

"Answer a fool according to his folly" (Proverbs 26:5).

The Atheist

He's this world's rube,
The quintessential boob—
Human answer to the mole,
Burrowed deep in his hole.

Exception to the rule,
He's the jest of April fool,
And to be quite frank,
His heart is rank.

According to the rule
Of how to treat a fool,
Since he's off his trolley,
Answer with like folly.

Scripture says they'd come—
The blind and the dumb.
Someone has to do it;
Let sleeping dogs pursue it.

Since he's buried his head,
It's gotta be said:
He shows his end
Where his head had been.

He's one of those guys
Who claim to be wise;
But he's really a joke,
Just blowin' smoke.

It's not that he's senile
But that he lives in denial.
He chimes, "No design."
Why, he's out of his mind!

With a brain like jelly,
He crawls on his belly.
With his eyes to the ground,
His thinkin' ain't sound.

Well, at any rate,
He's the chief ingrate.
He exclaims, "No God!" Poor brother!
I wonder if he has a mother.

As the quacks ruled the world of medicine in one age, are the scorn of the next, so has it been, and so will it be, with our atheistical savants and pretenders to science.
—C. H. Spurgeon, *An All Round Ministry*

They that deny a God, destroy man's nobility; for clearly man is of kin to the beasts by his body, and if he is not of kin to God by his spirit, he is a base and ignoble creature.

—Bacon

Nature is to thin a screen; the glory of the omnipresent God bursts through everything.

—Emerson

No one has ever died an atheist.

—Plato

Oh God, whom I have spent a life time denying . . . Save my soul, from hell!

—Robert Ingersoll

I would give worlds if I had them, that The Age of Reason had never been published. O Lord, help me! Lord JESUS CHRIST help me! . . No, don't leave; stay with me! Send even a child to stay with me; for I am on the edge of Hell here alone. If ever the Devil had an agent, I have been that one.

—Thomas Paine

All is dark, all is doubt.

—Edward Gibbon

The above rhyme is satire for one obvious reason: it is ludicrous to attempt to prove the obvious. However, there is another group of atheists that is larger in number and probably more despicable. These people are known as *practical atheists*. They claim to believe in God, but by their actions, they deny him, and doing so, they bring reproach upon the holy name of God. It would be difficult to determine which of the two is the most reprehensible. Of course, it is our desire and prayer that all people might repent and be saved.

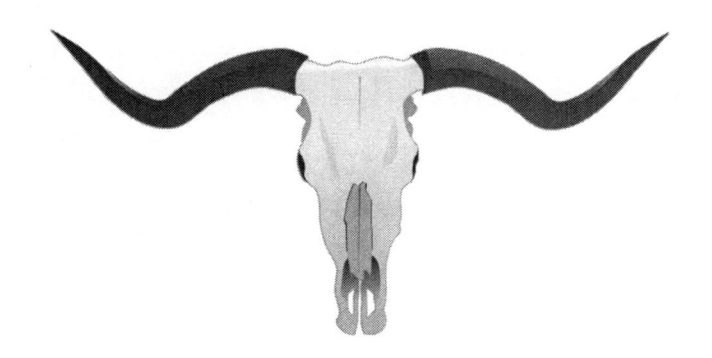

A True Story of Man without God

There was, in the old West, a fellow,
Proprietor of a bordello.
In his world of lust and vice,
Two things he observed with his eyes.

Seeing that things were amiss,
He described what he saw like this:
Men are fools—not wise—
And women are but devils in disguise.

"The prostitute reduces you to a loaf of bread, and the adulteress preys upon your very life" (Proverbs 6:26).

"The hearts of men, moreover, are full of evil and there is madness in their hearts while they live" (Ecclesiastes 9:3).

"They are like brute beasts, creatures of instinct, born only to be caught and destroyed, and like beasts they too will perish" (2 Peter 2:11-12).

People, created in the image of God, are also, in their flesh, akin to the animals. God designed humans to be guided by their God-like nature rather than their base animal instincts.

Fallen people prefer to please their fallen flesh rather than the higher desires of their spirits. The Bible tells us why that is so—people have fallen into a position of slavery, in which their lower natures rules over them.

Speaking to restored believers, the apostle Paul summed up what people are without God in their enslaved condition:

> Just as you used to offer the parts of your body in slavery to impurity and to ever-increasing wickedness, so now offer them in slavery to righteousness leading to holiness. When you were slaves to sin, you were free from the control of righteousness. What benefit did you reap at that time from the things you are now ashamed of? Those things result in death! But now that you have been set free from sin and have become slaves to God, the benefit you reap leads to holiness, and the result is eternal life. For the wages of sin is death, but the gift of God is eternal life in Christ Jesus our Lord. (Romans 6:19-23)

Due to our helpless condition, Jesus Christ came to rescue fallen humanity: "Christ died for sins . . . to bring you to God" (1 Peter 3:18).

Here I stand! I cannot do otherwise!

Justification by Faith Alone

Blessed doctrine of justification,
Reclaimed truth of the Reformation.
Justified by faith in God's dear Son,
By God's free grace and that alone.

There is now no condemnation
For the Savior's chosen nation,
For their debt's been fully paid;
All their sins on him were laid.

Being justified, we've perfect peace
From condemnation, sweet release.
Our debts forever paid in full—
Tell that to Satan if he should call.

Saved by grace, to the uttermost—
Not of works, lest we should boast.
Boasting is excluded, according to Paul,
On the basis of faith and not of law.

Tell Rome to scat with her unholy claims,
With her paternosters to multiple names.
Only one mediator between God and man:
Christ Jesus our Lord, no one else can.

Call on your Father up in the heavens;
Away with Rome's unholy inventions!
Straight to our Lord, and none beside,
It is he, not saints, that was crucified.

It is he, not dead saints, that rose again,
Who intercedes at God's right hand.
He is all you need; he's God's appointed one!
Do not insult the grace of God's dear Son.

"For it is by grace you have been saved, through faith—and this not from yourselves, it is the gift of God—*not by works*, so that no one can boast" (Ephesians 2:8-9).

"For there is one God and one mediator between God and men, the man Christ Jesus" (1 Timothy 2:5).

"Therefore, there is now *no condemnation* for those who are in Christ Jesus" (Romans 8:1).

"Therefore, since we have been justified through faith, we have peace with God through our Lord Jesus Christ" (Romans 5:1).

"Therefore he is able to save completely those who come to God through him, because he always lives to intercede for them" (Hebrews 7:25).

"Because Jesus lives forever, he has a permanent priesthood. Therefore he is able to save completely those who come to God through him, because he always lives to intercede for them" (Hebrews 7:24-25).

"Who will bring any charge against those whom God has chosen? It is God who justifies. Who is he that condemns? Christ Jesus, who died—more than that, who was raised to life—is at the right hand of God and is also interceding for us" (Romans 8:33-34).

"For in Christ all the fullness of the Deity lives in bodily form, and you have been given fullness in Christ" (Colossians 2:9-10).

There are only three possible ways by which one may be saved: grace alone, grace and works, or works alone. There are no other possible options. Rome opts for grace combined with works. For that very reason, the peace that Christ promises to the believer is impossible in the Roman system. The endless round of idolatry, superstition, traditional abominations, and prohibitions combine to make a settled peace with God impossible.

The apostle Paul nixed that whole idea in Romans 3:28: "For we maintain that a man is justified by faith apart from observing the law." That includes human laws as well as God's.

Below are some of the many human-made laws invented by the Roman Catholic fathers with the dates of their adoption.

Prayers for the dead—300
Beginning of the exaltation of Mary—431
Doctrine of Purgatory established—593
Title of Pope—607
Kissing the Pope's foot—709
Temporal power of the Popes—750
Worship of the cross, images, and relics—786
College of Cardinals established—727
Canonization of dead saints—995
Celibacy of the priesthood—1079
Sale of indulgences—1190
Transubstantiation—1215

Confession of sins to a priest—1215
Adoration of the wafer—1220
Purgatory proclaimed as dogma—1439
Tradition and Bible of equal authority—1545
Immaculate conception of Mary proclaimed—1854
Infallibility of the Pope—1870
Assumption of the Virgin Mary—1950
Mary proclaimed Mother of the church—1965

None of these are found in sacred Scripture. My Roman Catholic friends, it is time to ditch the baggage. Seek God as he is revealed in the Bible.

> Some indeed would have us show modesty, when we call the Pope Antichrist, who exercises tyranny over the souls of people, making himself a law giver equal to God. But we learn from this passage something far more—even that they are the members of Antichrist who willingly submit to be thus ensnared and that they thus renounce Christ when they connect themselves with a man who is not only a mortal, but also extols himself against God. It is, I say, prevaricating obedience, rendered to the Devil, when we allow any other than God himself to be a lawgiver to rule our souls.
> —John Calvin, Commenting on James 4:12

We may safely denounce an anathema on the whole theology of the Pope, for it wholly obscures the true light.
—John Calvin

The Christian Gospel is the message of grace. To a world deluged in a tidal wave of sin, the Christian presents a message of hope based not on what we can do for ourselves, but on what God has done for us through Jesus Christ. And to hearts longing for peace, the Gospel brings peace in its fullness. Lasting peace. Perfect peace. Peace purchased on Calvary's tree and sealed by the Holy Spirit.

Sola Gratia means "grace alone." God's grace is sufficient to bring about the salvation of His people. It needs no additions, no help along the way. God is powerful to save. And because of this, the believer can heartily agree with the second phrase, *Soli Deo Gloria,* "to God be the glory." God gets all the glory, for God has brought salvation to us. God did not simply make the plan available. God fully accomplished it and applies it by His Spirit. He alone receives honor for what He has done.

And it is because of this that I have peace with God. My salvation is His work and He has pledged to finish that work (Ephesians 1:14). I have peace today not because of my outer circumstances, my religious works, or anything else. I have peace with God because of Christ and Christ alone. I am accepted in Him. This is the Gospel of grace, and it is that Gospel I long to see all my brothers and sisters embrace, to His glory.

—James R. White, *The Roman Catholic Controversy*

The Indwelling

Gift of the Father's love to me,
I abide in Christ; he abides in me.
Espoused to Christ, and that forever—
Naught of earth or hell can sever.

"Christ in you, the hope of glory" (Colossians 1:27).

"You are in Christ Jesus" (1 Corinthians 1:30).

"I promised you to one husband, to Christ" (2 Corinthians 11:2).

"Never will I leave you" (Hebrews 13:5).

The reciprocal indwelling is one of the grandest truths in all of Scripture—an indissoluble relationship, an anchor of the soul, both sure and steadfast.

A Defense of Calvinism

In God's Word, dual truths are taught;
Neither must be set at naught.
One tells of God's owned sovereignty,
The other of man's responsibility.

For one to deny either reality
Is to act, in turn, dishonestly.
You must deal fairly with each,
For both the Scriptures teach.

God says to all sinners, "Welcome,"
Yet they willfully refuse to come.
What does the minister's prayer teach?
"Lord, make men willing as I preach.

"Draw sinners, O Lord, this very hour;
Demonstrate thy saving power."
Why even ask God's Spirit to call
If the sinner has power to do it all?

"All that the Father gives me will come,"
Christ declares in the gospel of John.
You prove your calling when you come—
When, by faith, you receive God's Son.

You, this day, are at the mercy of God.
His Spirit must draw, or you will not come.
This is not for you to understand;
Is it only for you to obey his command.

God commands all people to repent;
To you, today, the command is sent.
Do not harden your heart, as some,
And thus forever seal your doom.

Jesus said, "You must be born again."
That power has not been given to men.
This is where man's power ceases;
The Son gives life to whom he pleases.

All men are Calvinists on their knees;
When they rise, they say as they please.
They tell sinners, "God's done all he can do.
The rest, poor sinner, is up to you."

The blest, who God brings to salvation,
Have come to know their true condition;
They've cast themselves on mercy alone
And found true peace in God's dear Son.

The sovereign Lord is debtor to no man.
The fate of all, he holds in his hand.
Yet he has, in mercy, designed to save some—
Those who, in mercy, he has given his Son.

God showed no mercy to angels that fell,
But in his justice, consigned them to hell,
Kept in deep dungeons till judgment day,
When they will, in justice, get their pay.

Who is man to question God's will?
He may have, in justice, sent all to hell.
You've not learned mercy if you cavil today.
Tremble before him—submit while you may.

If you enter heaven, you can thank God's grace.
You can thank yourself if hell is your place.
You cannot blame God and his sovereign choice
While you willfully ignore the call of his voice.

Whosoever will may come to him today—
How many times have you turned him away?
How long must he on the rebels wait
Before he forever seals their fate?

"All that the Father gives me will come to me, and whoever comes to me I will never drive away" (John 6:37).

"No one can come to me unless the Father who sent me draws him" (John 6:44).

"The Son gives life to whom he is pleased to give it" (John 5:21).

"God did not spare angels when they sinned, but sent them to hell, putting them into gloomy dungeons to be held for judgment" (2 Peter 2:4).

"You refuse to come to me to have life" (John 5:40).

"He commands all people everywhere to repent" (Acts 17:30).

"Today, if you hear his voice, do not harden your hearts" (Hebrews 3:15).

"The Spirit and the bride say, 'Come!' And let him who hears say, 'Come!' Whoever is thirsty, let him come; and whoever wishes, let him take the free gift of the water of life" (Revelation 22:17).

The true Calvinist treats all of Scripture with due reverence. He accepts Scripture in its totality; he does not prune or deny anything that God has written. He, being of a humble and submissive spirit, does not submit God's Word to the bar of his natural reason. Conversely, he bends his will to the inspired Word. He is unwilling to part with even one syllable of divine truth. He treats the doctrines of salvation accurately and fully; he gives equal credence to God's sovereignty in divine election as well as to a person's responsibility to accept the gospel message on God's terms. He presents both, because the Bible plainly teaches both.

Calvinism gives due honor to God, the Holy Spirit. It honors him as the author of all things in regard to salvation. Salvation from start to finish is a divine work. The desire to come to God, the will to come, the power to come—all is the work of the Holy Spirit.

Total despair in regard to one's own abilities coupled with a total dependence upon God alone to accomplish a saving work within us is the very essence of Calvinism.

> When I was coming to Christ, I thought I was doing it all myself, and though I sought the Lord earnestly, I had no idea the Lord was seeking me. I do not think the young convert is at first aware of this . . . That God predestines, and yet that man is responsible, are two facts that few can see clearly. They are believed to be inconsistent and contradictory, but they are not. The fault is our week judgment.
> —C. H. Spurgeon, *A Defense of Calvinism*

The Crown of Life

Do not look for laurels
In your stand for God's truth;
Instead, you will be considered
Unloving, unkind, and uncouth.

God's truth is not at home
In this ungodly world;
If you take your stand for truth,
All hell will be unfurled.

You will be defamed
By men of earthly mind;
You will be called *anathema*
By the religious and refined.

Bigot is another name
They'll throw into your face—
And many other like things
While trav'ling through this place.

> So, pilgrim, do not lose heart;
> They did the same to him.
> You must follow in his train
> If you a crown would win.

"Dear friends . . . I felt I had to write and urge you to contend for the faith that was once for all entrusted to the saints" (Jude 3).

"If the world hates you, keep in mind that it hated me first. If you belonged to the world, it would love you as its own. As it is, you do not belong to the world, but I have chosen you out of the world. That is why the world hates you . . . 'No servant is greater than his master.' If they persecuted me, they will persecute you also. If they obeyed my teaching, they will obey yours also. They will treat you this way because of my name, for they do not know the One who sent me" (John 15:18-21)

"If you are insulted because of the name of Christ, you are blessed, for the Spirit of glory and of God rests on you" (1 Peter 4:14).

"They hated me without reason" (John 15:25).

"Blessed are you when people insult you, persecute you and falsely say all kinds of evil against you because of me. Rejoice and be glad, because great is your reward in heaven, for in the same way they persecuted the prophets who were before you" (Matthew 5:11-12).

"Blessed is the man who perseveres under trial, because when he has stood the test, he will receive the crown of life that God has promised to those who love him" (James 1:12).

> The reason why persecution awaits all those who are firmly resolved to adorn their confession with a truly Christian life is that in the midst of contradictions . . . they refuse either

to stop their ears or to cringe and compromise. Instead, they face the foe and challenge him to combat . . . The result is persecution, at times very bitter.

—William Hendriksen, *Commentary on 2 Timothy*

Today the fiercest enemies of the truth of God are the aliens in our communion. These are they who make believers in sound evangelical teaching look like strangers in the Churches.

—C. H. Spurgeon, *According to Promise*

I am coming soon. Hold on to what you have,
so that no one will take your crown.
—Revelation 3:11

Amen!
Come, Lord Jesus!